#11689

£12.50

22

KT-432-670

CREATIVE FLOWER ARRANGING

CREATIVE FLOWER ARRANGING

edited by Emma Callery

NEW
BURLINGTON
BOOKS

A QUINTET BOOK

Published by New Burlington Books
6 Blundell Street
London N7 9BH

ISBN 1-85348-350-8

This book was designed and produced by
Quintet Publishing Limited
6 Blundell Street
London N7 9BH

Creative Director: Terry Jeavons
Designers: Stuart Walden, Wayne Blades
Project Editor: Emma Callery

Typeset in Great Britain by
Central Southern Typesetters, Eastbourne
Manufactured in Hong Kong by
Regent Publishing Services Limited
Printed in Hong Kong by
Leefung-Asco Printers Limited

CONTENTS

CHAPTER 1:
THE BASICS

F LOWER ARRANGING *is a delightful pastime but before getting underway there are a few things which need to be kept in mind which are covered in this chapter. First it looks at the equipment – both basic and more specialized – and then goes on to consider where you can get your flowers from. A special look at seasonal flowers is followed by sections on conditioning techniques, containers and accessories and, finally, the four classic ways to arrange flowers, fresh or dried.*

LEFT *A fireplace in summer remains a focal point in the room. Here it is decorated with a pot of peonies, sweet williams, and roses.*

BASIC EQUIPMENT

A SELECTION of the correct tools and equipment can help tremendously in flower arranging to build up confidence and prevent frustration. If you start your collection with one or two basic pieces and add others as and when they are needed, or as your skills progress, the initial cost will not be too great. Choose well-designed equipment which should be easy and comfortable to use.

SCISSORS

There are several very good makes now available in varying price ranges. If possible try one or two for 'grip' and test the weight and balance in your hand. You may like a heavy tool – I prefer a light one. See if there is enough space for the fingers and thumb. Some of the so-called 'flower scissors' have very small rings which imprison your fingers. These are difficult to use and are therefore not recommended.

SHEARS

Those with long-blades such as shears used in the kitchen and by dressmakers, are also very handy for flower arrangers. They are ideal for cutting ribbon, fabric and fine wire. For the very heavy wire stems of some fabric flowers and foliage, you will need small secateurs, and for large woody branches, you will need gardening secateurs.

A SHARP KNIFE

This is an indispensable piece of equipment. It can be used for trimming all kinds of stems, and for pointing the tips so that they can be driven easily into foam. It can also be used for cutting floral foam and for removing thorns from rose

Basic equipment: 1 Well-designed watering can. 2 Packets of long-life powder for fresh flowers. 3 Oasis-fix, an oil-based fixative which can be removed from surfaces with white spirit. 4 Narrow-bladed knife sufficiently long to cut through soaked foam. 5 and 6 Stainless steel scissors and mini-secateurs, which are light, well-balanced and easy to handle. 7 Clear *adhesive tape about ⅜ in (10 mm) wide. 8 White vase. 9 Dry foam used for dried and fabric flower arrangements. 10 Large block of green foam – easily cut when soaked in water or a long-life solution. 11 Small cylindrical shape of green foam – a convenient size for plastic saucers and small containers. 12 Plastic water spray and mister. 13 Small plastic saucer. 14 Prongs.*

stems. This need not cost a lot of money – my favourite is an inexpensive little knife which is light and well-balanced, and, when sheathed, fits conveniently into a pocket or handbag. Moreover it can be finely sharpened to make an efficient tool.

FLORAL FOAMS

Floral foam is available in several makes but you should experiment with the various options to find out which one suits your particular needs. There are two distinct types: the green one used for fresh arrangements and the pale brown, dry one used exclusively for dried and fabric flower designs. The brown foam is solid and should never be soaked, the green variety is not solid enough to hold stems and should not be used dry.

Each type is available in several shapes and sizes. The large brick is made especially for large arrangements while cylinders and squares, which are about one-third of a large block in size, are useful for most small or medium-sized designs. One can, of course, cut a large block to the required size, but this will produce a certain amount of unavoidable waste. As each brand of foam varies, it is almost impossible to say precisely how long it will take for a particular size to become saturated. If you are using it for the first time, the following guide will be useful. Put the foam into a bowl or bucket of water and let it sink to the bottom. Allow 30 minutes for small blocks and up to two hours or longer, for large blocks. Floral foam is a fascinating substance. It is feather-light when dry and really heavy when it is completely saturated. Remember to cut this type of foam after it has been thoroughly soaked. To be certain it has taken in the maximum amount of water, cut right across the block and if the centre is still pale green, then it needs longer soaking.

FLOWER FOOD

This is sold either in small packets in powder form or as a liquid essence which must be diluted according to the directions on the bottle. The packets contain enough powder to make about 2 pints of solution. As well as the nourishment, which will noticeably prolong the life of your flowers, the preparation also contains a germ inhibitor specially formulated to keep the water pure. In fact, the manufacturers of some brands advise you not to change the vase water claiming that even summer flowers, such as scabious, larkspur and sweet william, which are renowned for polluting the water, will keep fresh in the solution. Use it for conditioning your flowers before arranging them and also for saturating the foam.

RECEPTACLES

It is advisable to keep a few plastic saucers handy which are useful for arranging designs in containers that will not hold water, such as baskets. However, since they have absolutely no decorative appeal, they should be regarded only as receptacles and not containers. They are available in varying sizes, in green, white or black.

OASIS-FIX

This is a dark green, malleable substance similar in texture to Plasticine, a modelling clay. It has a toffee-like appearance which never sets completely hard, but will stick almost any dry surfaces together. It is used extensively for attaching wired flowers to their bases, for securing a receptacle inside another container, and also for fixing candle-cups to vases or candle-sticks. It does not, however, adhere safely to glass or highly-glazed surfaces. As Oasis-fix is oil-based, it should not be applied directly to special wood surfaces such as wooden trays, table tops or fruit bowls for example. To prevent these surfaces from becoming stained, first apply a piece of adhesive tape or narrow masking tape, before putting a small amount of fixative on top.

It is a very useful substance for the majority of flower-arranging techniques. It can be bought by the roll and as it is used only in small amounts, a roll may last a very long time and fortunately does not deteriorate with keeping.

PRONGS

Prongs made from pale green plastic have four long pins on to which a block of foam is impaled for greater stability. They are inexpensive and cost very little to buy, and may be attached to the container with Oasis-fix. Remember that the base of the prong and the container must be completely dry. Unless the container is needed for something else, the prong can be left in place after discarding the flowers when it will be ready for the next arrangement. The Oasis-fix will never dry brick-hard, but the longer the prong is left attached, the firmer it becomes.

CLEAR ADHESIVE TAPE

Tape may be used for securing the foam to the container, especially for heavy designs, or if the arrangement has to be moved by vehicle. Smaller designs will be sufficiently firm if the foam is simply impaled on a prong, but for gladioli, dahlias, chrysanthemums and, in fact, all heavy and long-stemmed flowers, it is important to have the base really firmly anchored. Some flower arrangers use green or white Oasis-tape, but this is visible on the container, whereas clear adhesive tape will allow the colour of the container to show through. Both kinds of tape should be fixed to a completely dry surface.

A WATERING CAN

This is a very useful piece of equipment to have among your tools. It is quite indispensable for watering house plants, and also for adding water to flower arrangements when necessary. Even though you may previously have thoroughly soaked the foam and added water initially, there is bound to be some dehydration. As flowers should be taking in water all the time, it is essential that the foam is not allowed to dry out.

A SPRAY

A spray is very handy for giving your arrangement a final mist with clear water – obviously when you have spent time and trouble making the design you want it to last as long as possible. In addition to providing water for the stems a daily spray with a mister helps to keep the materials really fresh, especially if the room is warm or during hot weather.

SPECIAL EQUIPMENT

NONE OF THIS equipment is essential to the success of a simple flower design, but as your flower arranging skills improve and your interests widen, there are one or two special pieces of equipment that you may find useful to have on the shelf. It is better to acquire your equipment as you need it and not just because you think you ought to have it.

BELOW *Special Equipment: 1 Roll of water-resistant satin ribbon about 50 yds (47 m) long. 2 Polypropylene ribbon available in 100 yds (94 m) rolls. 3 A combined pinholder and small container. 4 Candle-cups. 5 and 6 Gold spray and colour spray. When using, it is advisable to wear plastic gloves for protection. 7 Clearlife. Two light coats are better than one generous coat. 8 One of several preparations for spraying onto green leaves to make them shine. 9 Floral tape used to cover wires and to seal the stem-end of support wires. 10 Stub wires, which can be bought in a variety of sizes and thicknesses. 11 Fine silver binding wire.*

RIBBONS

Ribbons can be an elegant addition to many flower arrangements and gifts so the more colours you have to choose from the better. The polypropylene or paper ribbon, in particular, is excellent for decorating bouquets. It is totally water-resistant and can be torn into strips of the required width. Woven ribbon, as opposed to the paper variety, is available in a wide range of colours and widths and is quite water-tolerant.

PINHOLDERS

Available in several sizes, they are useful for anchoring Japanese-style designs, and also for securing heavy branches. The illustration shows a pinholder and container made in one piece, which is intended to be placed in or on another base. The gold-spray finish makes it considerably more elegant than a plastic saucer.

CANDLE-CUPS

These are available in gold, black or white. They are small containers specially shaped with a 'foot' that can be fitted into the necks of bottles or candlesticks, or they can be secured to the top of narrow-necked containers.

COLOUR SPRAYS

Sprays may be needed now and again to complement a special colour scheme, such as gold, silver and bronze around Christmas-time. Old containers can be quickly revitalized with spray paint and new ones can be 'antiqued' using a combination of sprays.

Proprietary brand sprays can also be applied to living flowers and foliage, wood, plastic and even candles — to change or enhance their original colours. The sprays, however, should be used on living material with very great care.

CLEARLIFE

This is a colourless spray which helps to prolong the vase life of some fresh flowers. It prevents them from shattering, and flowers such as larkspur, delphinium, cornflower and eremurus, indeed, any that drop their petals, can be held a little longer with a light spray when the arrangement is completed.

STUB WIRES

These are useful for supporting flowers whose stems might become curved as they take up water.

FINE SILVER BINDING WIRE

Silver binding wire is used for fashioning ribbon bows, similar to the one illustrated. Make one loop and secure with a twist of silver wire. Make another loop securing it in the same place with the same length of wire. Continue adding loops until the bow is sufficiently full.

A less elaborate bow is made by folding the ribbon into a figure of eight and securing it across the centre with a taped wire. The floral tape will prevent the wire from rusting on to the ribbon, should it get wet, it also helps the wire to 'bite'.

FLORAL TAPE

This is used to cover non-silver wires. There are several varieties obtainable and one should experiment before deciding on any particular brand. It has been known to vary in performance in extreme climates.

WHERE TO GET YOUR FLOWERS

FLORISTS

When buying flowers, go into a florist shop and sniff hard: if you can smell decayed plant material, leave without buying. This is an almost foolproof guide that the florist is careless about conditioning and looking after his or her flowers.

When you do find a flower shop that smells sweet and clean, then start to inspect the stock. All plant material should look fresh and crisp, and be uncrumpled in appearance. It should look as though it still needed a little time to come out or open up. A good florist will condition his or her more expensive plant material, although it would not be economic to spend a lot of time on the cheap market bunches. The florist will protect the more fragile blooms from extremes of heat and cold, and those placed outside the shop in boxes will be sprayed with water when required.

Although there is a florist in most small towns, it is not the only place where you can buy flowers.

NURSERIES AND GROWERS

These generally specialize in only a few kinds of flowers intended for markets and florists, which means that the flowers must be fresh.

At a specialist nursery, such as that of a carnation grower, you can sometimes buy seconds. These are the side shoots of the flowers, not very big blooms, but ideal ones for flower arranging. Very often curved stems, split-ringed blooms, and so-called 'rogue colours' make a flower available as a second. As they are usually cheap, they are a good buy.

STREET VENDORS

Buying flowers from these sources depends a great deal on the characters who are actually selling the flowers. Those who are on the premises every day, or regularly every week, are anxious to please their customers. It is true that the flowers are usually more exposed to extremes of heat or cold, but these people generally only buy flowers that are not so affected by climatic conditions. They don't carry such large supplies, and visits to the flower market are usually very frequent. You should get value for money, providing you make sure the material is crisp and fresh.

Often you will find relatively inexpensive flowers in this way – don't dismiss these as a bad buy, for when there is a glut in the market these vendors are able to turn their stock over quickly. At the end of the day, and particularly on weekends, these vendors generally sell off bunches cheaply to avoid having left-over flowers (which by Monday will be unsaleable). This can prove to be a bonus, as well as a good buy, for you.

GREENGROCERS AND GROCERY STORES

Some grocers sell flowers as a sideline. If the produce is local, it is usually quite good. However, be careful of the multiple stores, or chains, who are often guilty of dumping boxes of flowers in exposed positions where they are subject to extremes of cold or heat.

For instance, I wouldn't purchase flowers such as violets or freesias that have been exposed to a hard frost, so do be cautious when buying all but the hardy species such as chrysanthemums. Where flowers have some shelter, such as a side awning, they are usually protected sufficiently.

As these flowers are generally cheaper than those at a florist, they can be useful when you want to brighten up the home.

GARDEN BUNCHES

When out in the country in the summer, you will often see signs outside small gardens offering 'Fresh-cut Flowers'. These are often gardeners selling their surplus stock. Usually presented as mixed bunches, they are great for making a variegated flower arrangement, and as the bunches are usually generous, you can make a massed design.

Often you will discover that these gardeners like to talk about their flowers, and I have received some good gardening tips in these places, as well as pretty flowers. The flowers themselves are generally standing in buckets of deep water in the shade, and those I have bought have always been nice and fresh.

OPPOSITE *Specialist nurseries and garden centres generally stock only a few kinds of flowers intended for markets and florists. You may be able to buy seconds at a cheaper price, but still fresh and of good quality.*

GROWING FLOWERS IN THE GARDEN

IT IS WELL WORTH growing plants that are not easily obtained at the florist. I only have a small garden so I grow white daffodils in it instead of yellow ones, which are easy to get elsewhere. I grow Rembrandt, Viridiflora and lily-flowered tulips, not the more easily bought cottage types. They do not take up any more room, and the bulbs are not that much more expensive than the other, more common kinds, and you will find that you get more interested in your arrangements by doing this.

I like the foliage of geraniums, but I just can't spare the room for them in the garden, so I attach them onto the wall in individual pots. This allows me a little more picking material, and is an idea that could easily be adapted by those of you who live in apartments. City dwellers who have a balcony can grow quite a few subjects in tubs or pots. The larger tubs will take quite substantial shrubs, and if you choose an evergreen subject, you will have plant material to pick from even in the winter months. Underplant with small bulbs or annuals.

I have plants that are special favourites of mine. Of the perennials I include lady's mantle, or *Alchemilla mollis,* a lovely foam of lime-green flowers that goes with just about everything; yarrow, or *Achillea filipendulina* 'Coronation Gold', which makes an impressive garden plant (plus the flat yellow heads dry beautifully), and various heuchera – I have the coral and the red varieties, both of which are useful for pointed material in arrangements.

I also grow quite a few roses, and there is no doubt that the most prolific in my garden is the 'Queen Elizabeth' variety, a pink rose which gives both

Antirrhinum.

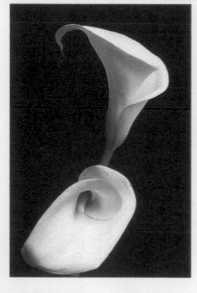

Arum lily.

clusters and single blooms. It goes on blooming for so long that I have even picked flowers from it on Christmas Day. There are, of course, many varieties of hybrid tea roses to choose from with a vast colour range.

I like the curious little *Rosa viridiflora,* and one year I was able to pick flowers from it every single month of the year. I don't grow the old-fashioned ones; I would love to, but they are generally large and not repeat-flowering.

Lilies are a great favourite, and with so many colours and varieties to use, just pick the ones you like best. Don't forget to plant something for autumn and winter use. I would recommend nerines, which usually flower in October, along with with *Schizostylis coccinea,* or Kaffir lily, a flower that is like a small gladiolus. Dahlias usually last well into the autumn and stick around until the first frost. Chrysanthemums are long-lasting in the garden, and I have found that zinnias and African marigolds last until the frosts.

For real winter flowers, *Iris unguicularis* is a little gem that braves the cold weather. I start to pick mine a couple of weeks into winter, and I can do so for about four more months. Also winter-flowering are heathers; winter jasmine, which provides yellow sprays in the sort of weather you feel it couldn't survive; snowdrops, small but charming, and *Iris reticulata* and *I. danfordia,* both of which will provide winter flowers from mid- to late winter.

If you have room, some small trees can give good material for cutting. Pittosporum – in green, green and white, or bronze – is useful, but it does require a sheltered position except in extreme southern locations. Another small tree I love is *Garrya elliptica,* both for its long tassels in mid- to late winter and its evergreen foliage.

If you have a garden you can really enjoy yourself with flower arrangements. Not only can you grow what you need, but you can experience the pleasure of watching your garden grow, season after season.

This section will be directed at those of you with small gardens; if you are lucky enough to have a very large garden, you can just add things as you choose.

Small gardens should include a few shrubs and foliage plants. You will have to look upon buying shrubs as a long-term investment, although it is possible to take cuttings from a number of shrubs. Also, if you go to classes or to a flower club, see if you can swap something you have for someone else's plant material. Shrubs that are easy to propagate are the weigelas – the golden and the variegated ones are very useful. I have rooted rosemary, privet, rue, some of the hebes and Japanese honeysuckle without special equipment. All of these shrubs are very useful to grow; they, along with ivies, should afford you plenty of background materials to play with.

The ivy that I like best is the one called 'Gold Heart', a very pretty one which has lovely sprays and larger leaves to use at the base of the arrangement. It is deep green with a bright yellow centre, and has an added advantage, in that you can pick it in the winter. I grew my original one from a cutting, and I must admit that it took a long time to get going, but it was worth the wait.

If you have a shady part of the garden, grow ferns and hostas. They thrive in the shade, and if you grow only three varieties of fern and three of hostas it will give you a great deal of material to pick from once the plants are established. Personally I loathe privet hedges, but a golden

Cowslip.

Lily-of-the-valley.

Foxgloves.

privet grown as a specimen shrub is quite another thing, for not only does it look lovely but also it provides a great deal of material for cutting. I would advise growing those shrubs that suit your own area's soil conditions, always taking into account whether you are in the shade or the sun.

If you have a small garden, it is much better to grow any suitable plants that grow well in your area. If you see the plants you want to grow flourishing in neighbours' gardens, they are quite likely to do well in yours. Go for the easier plants rather than those that are difficult to grow, but if you want to experiment with more temperamental specimens, the best thing to do is to grow them in pots. You can then move them around so that they are subject to favourable growing conditions.

If your garden has a lot of space in it, annuals and half-hardy annuals are a quick way to obtain plant material for picking while you are waiting for the perennials to mature.

A good trick with small gardens is to see how much you can get from one plant. Two annuals that I find useful are candytuft, which provides flowers with a pretty green seedhead that will also take up glycerine; and nigella, which similarly has attractive flowers and a green seed-head that can be glycerined or dried. Honesty (*Lunaria annua*, or satinpod), a biennial, is another great plant for giving a variety of plant material, especially if you can get hold of the one with varie-gated leaves. You then have foliage, flowers and green seedpods, which at this stage can be glycerined or dried by air-hanging, or you can leave them on the plant until the pods are brown and then carefully peeled, revealing the familiar silvery discs. You can also save the outer husks to create made-up flowers.

SEASONAL FLOWERS

WHEN YOU BUY flowers, it is nearly always best to do so when they are in season, for not only are they plentiful and at their peak of beauty, but they are also at their lowest price. It is possible, for example, to buy daffodils in mid-winter, but these are much more expensive than the flowers you can buy in the spring, and often not as fresh and attractive as the seasonal variety.

The seasons do vary – a cold or wet spell can delay the time the blooms would normally be available – so it is not possible to list available flowers with complete accuracy. However, covering the times of year with the reasonably priced flowers you can purchase within them, in normal seasons the following are what you would expect to find (bear in mind that seasons do overlap):

MID-WINTER
Chrysanthemums, snowdrops, anemones, mimosa, violets and tulips.

LATE WINTER
Same as mid-winter, with some daffodils starting to be reasonable.

EARLY SPRING
Daffodils, tulips, anemones and hyacinths. Irises come into the shops now, and although a bit more expensive than the other flowers mentioned, they do seem to last longer at this time of year.

MID-SPRING
Tulips, daffodils, irises, narcissi, long-stemmed French anemones, hyacinths, ranunculas and wallflowers (Cheiranthus species, or gillyflower). Also small bulb flowers are occasionally found, depending on the florist that you use.

Daffodil.

Liatris.

LATE SPRING
Daffodils are mainly finished, although I have on occasion bought them in the very early spring. Late tulips are still available, and irises are normally as inexpensive and abundant as they are likely to get.

EARLY SUMMER
Sees the start of the warm-weather flowers, with cornflowers, lilies, sweet williams, carnations, larkspur, antirrhinum (snap-dragon) and roses available at reasonable prices.

MID-SUMMER
This time of year brings scabious, gypsophila (baby's breath), alstroemeria, cornflowers, larkspur, roses, spray carnations and carnations. Sweet peas and lilies are usually at their peak at this time of year. Bunches of statice and helichrysum start to appear in the shops; since these can be dried for winter use, you can use them fresh and perhaps dry half of your bunch for winter use.

LATE SUMMER
Scabious are usually over, but most of the other flowers that were available in mid-summer are still plentiful, in addition to marigolds, gladioli and dahlias, which start to appear at this time. Asters are available toward the end of the period. Other flowers such as statice and rhodanthe are sometimes available in limited quantity. I should add that it is possible to buy dried material all the year round, but I always prefer to dry my own.

EARLY AUTUMN
Dahlias are in full swing, with a great variety of form and colour, and chry-

santhemums are appearing cheaply again; gladioli are still available but starting to go up in price. Asters are a good buy.

MID-AUTUMN

Chrysanthemums start to come in bunches and are very good buys at this time of year. Spray chrysanthemums are good value as well. Look out for Chinese lanterns for drying. Other flowers are available but starting to get more expensive. The amaryllis-like nerine and *Schizostylis coccinea*, or Kaffir lily, are reasonably priced.

LATE AUTUMN

It's still chrysanthemum season, but luckily they come in a wide variety of colours and forms, so there is no danger of getting bored with them. Try the rayonnante or anemone-flowered type for a change. Anemones are also available.

EARLY WINTER

Apart from our friend the chrysanthemum and possibly small flowers like anemones, this is the most expensive time of year for flowers; but take heart, for if you buy a small bunch of freesias or some of the first daffodils, they will last much longer at this time of year. Sugar-pine foliage is also a good buy, and can form an impressive background for north-temperature holiday arrangements. Holly and mistletoe are available, but the quality does vary according to the weather conditions prevalent during the year. Cones that have been gathered over the year can be wired and glittered, frosted or painted to blend in with holiday decorations.

Freesias and carnations are beautiful spring flowers to use in an arrangement.

CONDITIONING TECHNIQUES

YOUR MATERIAL WILL presumably come from either the florist's shop, or the garden, or both. In either case, it will need a certain amount of care and attention before being arranged. This is called conditioning.

GARDEN FLOWERS

These can be cut in the early morning or late evening. The moment a stem is severed from the parent plant, its life support is cut off. In order that the flower or foliage can continue to survive compensate by putting it in water, preferably in a flower food solution. Not even this can give it all the nourishment it was getting from the root system, but it will help to prolong its freshness.

To condition garden material, prepare a container of water before cutting, adding the correct amount of flower food. A deep plastic bucket is the most useful but it need not be completely filled. It has recently been established that most flowers do not require deep water, the ideal depth being about 7 in (20 cm). Bulb-grown flowers are an exception and need only 3–4 in (8–10 cm). As you cut the flowers strip off any leaves low down on the stems. Always carry them head downwards as this helps to retain any moisture in the stems. Before standing the material in water, use a very sharp knife and trim each stem end to a sharp point. The exposed angle will offer a larger surface to the water than if the stem were cut straight across.

Any stems carrying thorns, such as roses and some shrubs should be trimmed, not only for easy handling while you are arranging, but to prevent the thorns from hooking into other flowers. To de-thorn roses, hold your knife blade

Cutting the stem at the conditioning stage. Stems of garden flowers should be cut at a sharp angle and with a sharp knife before being stood in water.

almost flat against the stem and 'chop' each thorn away. Alternatively, the thorns can be pulled off one by one between finger and thumb but this is a very slow process. Garden roses rarely refuse to take up water. Among flowers which may need special attention are lilac, poppies, zinnias and marigolds. Lilac will take up water more readily if most of the foliage is stripped off. It also has very woody stems and prefers to be conditioned in hot water.

Poppies are supposedly very short-lived, but if the stems are instantly plunged into very hot water, or the end is sealed over a flame, they will last for several days. Their decorative quality is outstanding so special care is well worth the trouble.

Zinnias and large marigolds sometimes droop their heads just below the flower. The stems are hollow and seem incapable of supporting such magnificent flowers. Insert a wire inside the stem until it reaches the flower-head — when upright the flower will take up water happily.

Apart from a shortage of water, draughts are a flower's enemy, so set your material in a cool, draught-free place to rehabilitate before being arranged. Flowers do not really thrive in direct sunlight, particularly where the heat is concentrated through glass. But it is surprising how tolerant they are once they have been properly conditioned.

An appealing, well-balanced design should ideally include both buds and open flowers. However, a fully matured flower does not have as long a vase life as a younger bud or flower. This should be taken into consideration when planning the arrangement. So often the largest flower is set into the heart of a design, and when it fades the arrangement looks empty and disappointing.

Bulb-grown flowers are wonderfully trouble-free, though if they are cut *too* young, that is, if the bud is just too tight, the flower will never develop to its full beauty.

Flowers should never be cut in full sunshine. The best time is early morning or after sundown.

MATERIAL FROM A FLOWER SHOP

Flowers will already have been conditioned but the stems will callous over in transit and should therefore be re-cut. They can then be treated as flowers from the garden although they will not need to stay as long in the conditioning bucket before being arranged.

Most shop flowers will have been in transit for several hours, indeed even a few days during which time they have been without water. However, good conditioning will usually 'set them on their feet again', although some flowers,

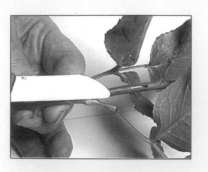

1 To condition and de-thorn roses, *take a sharp knife and cut off any leaves which are growing on the lower part of the stem.*

2 *With the blade of your knife almost flat against the stem, carefully remove the thorns at the base of the stem to give about a 5 in (13 cm) length of stem to hold.*

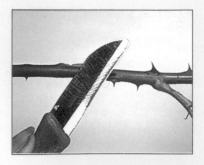

3 *With the knife blade at the same angle, and facing away from you, slice the remaining thorns off, finishing at the head.*

Two pieces of gypsophila cut from the same branch being treated with a fixative spray. One of these stems was then placed in a flower food solution, the other in plain water. The benefit gained from the flower food treatment was quite noticeable.

such as roses, occasionally refuse to take up water. In this case, re-cut the stem and stand the rose in hot water. This will soften the stem tissues and the flower will probably take up water within a few moments. Or, stand it in a carbonated liquid such as fizzy lemonade. The fizz will drive the liquid up the stem while the sugar content feeds the flower.

Total immersion is used for most broad leaves. They respond well to being literally 'drowned' for several hours, after which they will last well for many days in the design. Hosta, caladium, dieffenbachia, wild arum, *Begonia rex,* geranium and numerous other flowers benefit from this apparently drastic treatment. Roses that refuse to drink usually revive if totally submerged for several hours.

Heavy wooded stems such as chrysanthemums, branches of trees, flowering trees and shrubs should, if possible, be broken at the stem end with your fingers. If the branch is too tough to break this way, cut it with secateurs and condition in very hot water.

The concept of hammering hardwood stems to pulverize the end has been rejected on the basis that the fringed stem that results is an ideal breeding ground for bacteria.

While on the subject of bacteria, it is worth pointing out that diseased materials should never be used and that all the containers you use for either conditioning or arranging should be kept perfectly clean. From time to time, they should be sterilized and cleaned thoroughly. Similarly your tools will also need to be cleaned. The blades of knives and scissors should be polished with steel wool and regularly sharpened.

FORCING FLOWERS AND OTHER PLANT MATERIAL

In mid-winter, I always bring some sprays of forsythia indoors to force, even though at this time of the year they resemble little more than knobbly sticks. I choose the stems with plenty of small buds up the sides, then place them in about 2 in (5 cm) of cold water and stand them in the kitchen window. I change the water frequently so that the stems don't become soggy, and usually I put the ends that have been in water under the cold tap to prevent any build-up of slime.

In a month or so, the forsythia are usually in full flower. As soon as they start to show colour I arrange them, and then I bring in another lot, enabling me to have a succession of winter blossoms. In the garden they seldom start to show colour until very late in the winter, so that means I have a whole extra month in which to appreciate the yellow flowers.

I also bring in stems of flowering currant (of the Ribes genus). The treatment is the same as for forsythia, but I usually banish this plant to the greenhouse, since I don't like the smell of it when it is newly picked. When they appear, the current flowers are a very pale pink, in fact, almost white, but the plant has pretty leaves and looks quite attractive when used with tulips.

Hazel catkins are brought in mid-winter and soon open up in the warm. These are useful for landscape arrangements, or even on their own in a pottery vase. Catkins of the alder are the next to come in, and if the buds of the pussy willow look fairly plump, I bring them in as well.

You may be able to force the catkins and pussy willow about two to three weeks earlier than they will appear outside, but at that time of the year, when flowers are at their scarcest (and most expensive), I think it is worth the effort. Pussy willow makes a pretty framework for a few anemones or a bunch of daffodils, and because you can curve it in your hands, you can make outlines for winter moderns. Curve by placing your thumbs under the willow, and then gently pressing down along the stem until the desired arc is obtained.

Foliage showing fat buds can also be forced. Hawthorn, one of the first to come out, has pretty leaves that nicely complement spring flowers. When the forsythia you have forced has finished flowering, you can take off the spent flowers and let the leaves develop, again providing attractive foliage for filling in the gaps in your spring arrangements.

1 To condition your flowers and foliage, fill a bucket with lukewarm water and add a teaspoon of sugar.
2 Strip all lower leaves away from the stem.
3 Recut the stem end and then place in the mild sugar solution for two hours or overnight.

1

2

3

HOLDING AND FIXING FLOWERS

Asuccessful flower arrangement depends on how firmly it is anchored to the base. There are several methods of preparing containers and bases: floral foam is now so much a part of the flower arranger's basic equipment that it is difficult to remember how arrangements were ever made without it. But, efficient though it is, it is certainly not the only way of supporting the material, in fact, some flowers prefer to be directly in water whenever possible. Proteas, in particular, last far longer if they can stand in deep water, while gladioli, although they last quite well when arranged in foam, really prefer to have their stems in water.

Wire mesh, pinholders, moss, sand and cut branches all help to support the material and your choice of method must be dictated by the size and type of design, as well as the material being used.

Many arrangers like to use mesh as well as foam. This is a very valid method, particularly for rather large heavy material. Mesh used alone should be crumpled to fit the shape of the container, preferably with some left well above the rim. If you press it in too low, you will have no support for your lateral stems. Even though it may seem fairly firm, it is advisable to secure it to the rim of the container with adhesive tape or string.

If you are using a container with an extremely high glaze, or made of glass, the Oasis-fix will not adhere firmly enough. The solution is to fold a piece of tissue or paper kitchen towel and use it as a small non-skid mat for the foam. The block should then be fixed firmly with adhesive tape.

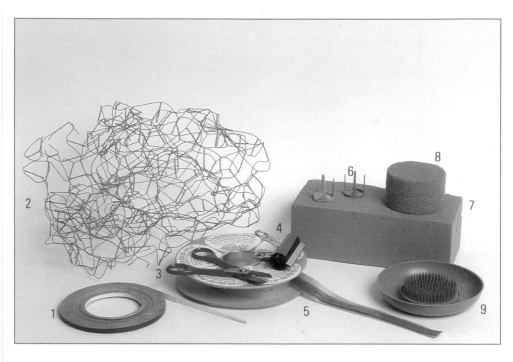

ABOVE *Basic equipment for flower arranging includes:* **1** *Floral tape.* **2** *Wire mesh.* **3** *Mini-secateurs.* **4** *Bulldog clip.* **5** *Oasis fix.* **6** *Oasis pin.* **7** *Large block of green foam.* **8** *Dry foam for dried and fabric arrangements.* **9** *Small oasis bowl.*

Sand is sometimes used at the base of a container for dried flowers. But be very careful, for sand is heavy and if too much is used, it could make the base of the vase fall out.

If you are totally without any support mechanism, cut some stems or small branches to the depth of the vase. Almost fill the aperture and they will give the necessary support, though a design with spreading lateral lines would not be practical.

In deciding the size of foam, the main thing to remember is that once you have inserted a stem you have made a hole which obviously weakens the block. If you have never used foam, cut a piece you feel will take every stem comfortably. If your container has a round opening, then choose a square piece of foam, and vice versa. This allows for a better fit and there will be a space left to insert the spout of the watering can for adding more water.

The depth of the foam is easier to estimate. Since most arrangements have some lateral stems, make sure the foam stands at least 1 in (2 cm) above the rim of the container otherwise you will be trying to insert stems into mid-air.

Pinholders of varying sizes are useful for shallow containers. They are very heavy and need no fixative to hold them in position. They can also be used together with wire mesh for larger arrangements that include heavy

Soaked floral foam will need to be secured to a shallow 'open' base. It can be impaled on prongs which have been attached to a plastic saucer by Oasis-fix. Both prongs and container must be clean and dry if the Oasis-fix is to adhere firmly.

An old-fashioned wire support in a wide-mouthed urn. Both support and urn pose problems: the urn requires a very large number of flowers for a balanced design, and the wire support (superseded by more modern floral foam and mesh) is very difficult to handle. Definitely a container to leave well alone.

branches and flowers with large stems, for example, arum lilies. They will also tolerate foam, but much prefer to be directly in water.

Large containers, of course, present a greater challenge than smaller ones. For example, the type of brass container sometimes used in churches becomes impossibly heavy if filled with water, while the neck is often rather small. One solution to the problem is to locate a smaller container that will effectively slot into the neck thus forming a kind of inner lining. Alternatively, a large candle-cup may be used though even the largest size may not be big enough to hold a piece of foam large enough to support a really large design.

Each time you make an arrangement, try to keep the size of foam used down to a minimum. Although it is far easier to design into a large block, it needs a lot of material to mask it which is, at least, time-consuming. But never make it so

small as to risk the foam collapsing. Like many other skills, there are certain guide-lines to follow, but eventually, one becomes experienced in what your tools — in this case, the foam — can do for you.

Remember, before you begin a design, to add water to the container as soon as you are satisfied that the base is firm. It is far easier at this stage than when all the material is in place.

In order to travel with a design, it is safer to pour the water out when the arrangement is finished, and take a small can with you to refill the container once it is in place. The well-soaked foam will keep the flowers fresh for many hours but in a warm atmosphere you will get a longer vase life from the flowers if the container is kept filled with water.

USING FOAM AND MESH

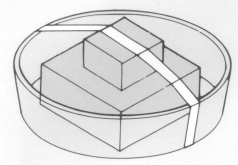

A foam base should stand at least 1 in (2 cm) above the rim of your container. Deep bowls may need two pieces of foam stacked to achieve sufficient height. A second smaller piece may be impaled on the first and the two secured firmly to the container with adhesive tape.

Mesh is particularly useful as extra support for heavy designs. It should be fixed to your container with a loop of adhesive tape secured on either side. With a large container, the mesh may need to be secured in three places.

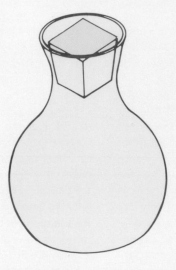

It is important to cut soaked foam to a size that will fit securely into the neck of your container. A square piece should be wedged into a round neck and a round piece into a square neck. This ensures a good fit and leaves room for adding more water when necessary.

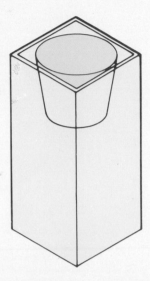

A large pot of this kind (LEFT) and also in the diagram (ABOVE) can be made smaller by inserting a smaller pot into its neck. This solves the problem of securing the foam sufficiently well to carry a big design. It also reduces the amount of water – and therefore of additional weight – needed to keep the flowers and foliage fresh.

USING FIXATIVES

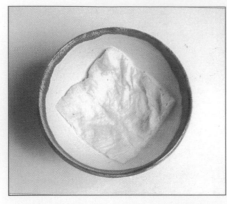

1 *Oasis-fix will not adhere well to a highly-glazed surface. A damp tissue placed in the base of this shallow compote will stop floral foam from sliding.*

2 *The foam, resting on the paper, is fixed with adhesive tape. The two pieces of stem seen here will prevent the tape from biting into the foam.*

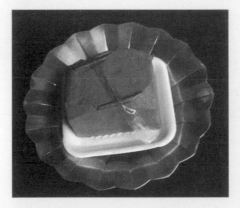

3 *Here soaked foam has been laid on a polystyrene tray to protect the surface of the silver container. The foam is firmly secured to the tray with adhesive tape.*

4 *For display purposes, a damaged leaf can be patched on the underside with a section from another leaf. Use a little glue, plus a little care, to complete the disguise.*

For this contemporary free-style arrangement a large pinholder is sufficiently heavy to sit firmly in the shallow highly-glazed dish. The decorative stones help to mask the pinholder so that the minimum of foliage is needed. Each stem should be held very close to the pinholder and impaled firmly.

CONTAINERS AND ACCESSORIES

To a flower arranger, any container that is capable of holding water or floral foam can be pressed into use. There is no need to rush out and buy expensive containers, since there are many things about the house that you can use – jugs, coffee mugs, baking dishes, ashtrays, even that old teapot with a broken lid. I'm sure that if you have a good rummage round you will find any number of things you can put into service.

You should purchase a little device called a candle cup, preferably one made of metal – it can be inserted into the top of candlesticks and bottles to give you a raised container. Wind a little piece of adhesive clay sausage-like around the rim of the candlestick or bottle and push the nozzle into the hole. Tape the cup to the bottle for extra holding power. Metal is best since metal sticks much better to glass and china than plastic does, although the plastic variety is fine for wooden items.

If you want to add to your collection of containers without spending too much money, go to charity (thrift) shops, jumble (rummage) sales, car boot sales, swap meets, flea markets and junk shops, where you may well be able to find something that you can use, if not an outright treasure. Just make sure that it has a good shape and is *in* good shape – you can always give the receptacle a coat of paint if you don't like the colour.

One of my favourite containers came from a summer fair. It was in the most hideous shade of green you could imagine, and would have clashed wildly with any foliage used in it. But still I took it home, where I found a few old tin cans of paint in the shed with a scant scraping of useable paint at the bottom. I had just enough dark brown to paint the container completely. Then I trickled a very small amount of beige paint on top of the brown, brushing it in with a light downward stroke. I was most pleased with the result, which gave the vessel an interesting pottery glaze. I'm telling you this story to remind you that flower arrangers seldom throw anything away!

MAKING YOUR OWN CONTAINERS

A good way of saving money – and unleashing your creativity – is to have a go at making your own containers. The basic ingredients for doing this are yoghurt cartons, empty tin cans, fabrics, leftover pieces of braid, stick-on plastic, bleach and liquid detergent bottles, paint, glue and other finishing materials.

The easiest container is a simple bleach bottle – cut off the nozzle end, level off the top and paint it. Or, if straight-sided, cover it with glued-on fabric. Cut the fabric about 1 in (2.5 cm) larger than the perimeter of the container and glue under ¼ in (6 mm) on one long side so that

Glass, porcelain and plastic containers can all be used effectively.

this can be stuck on top of the other long side. Finish off the top and bottom with a length of braid.

Bind string around a tin can to give it an interesting texture; you only need to glue the ends. Cover a bleach bottle (one of the smooth straight ones) with a piece of contact paper or other adhesive-backed plastic material. It will take you all of five minutes to do. For these containers the width used for covering shelves is sufficient. You can also make a quick base to match. If it is round or oval, snip the plastic to the rim at about ½ in (1.3 cm) intervals before pressing down to the underside; this will give a neat finish to the base.

With tall containers that you have made, the simplest form of mechanics is leftover floral foam three-quarters of the way up, and a new piece in the remainder. However, should you wish to use a small pinholder, you will need a small tin can that fits snugly into the top of the container; then fill the container with made-up filler compound to the bottom of the tin can, making sure that the can is level with the rim of the container. Allow the filler to dry out before putting the tin into the final position. Small plastic containers such as those used for ice cream or cream can be stuck together with a strong glue. Stick them together at their bases (one being upside-down), and when the glue has dried paint in the colour of your choice. If you want, finish off with narrow Russian braid at the top and bottom.

Try different textures for covering cans and bottles. For instance, lightly apply filler compound over the surface, then rough it up or make a pattern on it with a fork. Or, cover the container with glue and roll it in sand and sawdust. Some of the results may be a bit fragile, but at least they will give you a variety of containers to play with.

A medium-sized roasting pan can be painted black on the outside and blue-green on the inside, which is quite attractive to use for water scenes. There are a number of cheap plastic containers on the market, and it is often worth buying these to repaint in the shade of your choice, or you could add decorative mouldings before painting to give a container a distinctive period look.

An urn with grooves can be painted in moss green, its grooves lightly touched up with black paint to give it an antique look. Or you can add a tin can the same size as the base of the container, which you can then cover with a remnant of matching velvet and finish with narrow braid. It will add both height and elegance to an inexpensive container.

It is also possible to buy screw-on bowls, which you can adapt to a table lamp by simply removing the light fittings and screwing in the bowl. Those with figurines, marble or mock onyx look attractive.

Shells are another good form of container, and even the smaller ones are fine for dainty arrangements. With most shells a piece of floral foam cut to fit will hold your plant material.

Containers can be made of wood providing you are handy with a saw. However with wooden containers it is important to remember that they will need a lining of some sort to enable them to hold water.

Using a figurine in arrangements is a good way of cutting down the number of flowers needed.

I have only mentioned the very simple containers that anyone can make, but those of you who enjoy making things can experiment with your own ideas. Those of you adept at basketry and pottery can make up your own designs by drawing rough ideas before you begin.

CHOOSING CONTAINERS AND ACCESSORIES

At some stage in your flower-arranging career you will of course want to acquire more containers than those you have made or adapted from items about the house.

If you are buying an expensive container, first make sure that you like it, for you will have to live with it; and be sure the colour is something that will blend with plant material. My own choices would be moss or leaf green, brown or grey. Although white and black are neutral, black doesn't show soft colours to advantage, and unless all-white flowers are to be used, white containers can dominate the flowers.

As to style, it is a good idea to collect different sorts of designs. An open container with a good area inside for water scenes is useful, as is a modern container, perhaps one with two openings that can increase the ways you can use it. Also good to have on hand are a basket with a handle, an attractive box, and a cherub- or other figurine-shaped vessel for more formal arrangements. Containers with a pedestal in china or metal are useful, and perhaps one of opaque glass, since its opacity makes it much easier to hide the mechanism.

An accessory is an object that is not made of plant material and with careful use they can enhance an arrangement considerably.

Other unusual containers may be obtainable from time to time; some have limited use but are fun to experiment with. Antique containers are useful if you enjoy doing period designs, but these can be very expensive. Items such as Victorian epergnes are very costly, as are vases with crystal drops. I have, however, seen reproductions of some of the antique designs which can still give the right feeling to vintage designs.

Other containers which are lovely to own are the spelter (a kind of zinc) figurines which were used for lamps and have been adapted for usage as containers. The arms on these are usually a bit vulnerable, so care should be taken when carrying them from place to place. Marble containers should always have a supplementary container inside, as the damp can spoil them. Silver is easily scratched,

so, again, a lining of some sort is advisable to prevent this.

With accessories the choice is endless; from plastic figurines, which are inexpensive, to Royal Doulton statuettes, which are much more highly priced, all are suitable.

Anything you enjoy can be used when arranging at home for your own personal pleasure, such as a carved wooden elephant or a china swan; but for shows it must be appropriate to the theme. But in both cases, keep away from the gimmicky and garish, for they will do your flowers no favours.

LOOKING AT BASES

Bases in flower arrangements serve to add colour, give a design visual weight and added texture, provide further interpretation, raise the design and protect furniture from water spillage.

Any design that you make should have all its parts in harmony with each other, so avoid putting anything under an

arrangement without considering the final effect. As an example, if I were to put a red satin base under a green-dominated landscape arrangement, it would totally lack in harmony, just as would placing an elegant arrangement in fine china on a wooden slab.

From an economic point of view, a base can add interest to your flowers without being too expensive a proposition. For a simple, attractive base, obtain a set of cake boards in three different sizes; those measuring 6–9 in (15–23 cm) should give you a good start. Simply take remnants of fabric cut about 1½ in (3.8 cm) wider than your board all around; make a single hem around your fabric, leaving a small opening to thread through with narrow elastic drawn up to fit the base. You now have a removable cover that you can make up in different colours to go with your arrangement.

The bases can be used separately or in conjunction with one another. Straw table mats and those made of thin cane are useful, and offcuts of hardboard or chipboard can be used after being cut to size and covered with stick-on plastics. The woodgrain, pebble or marble designs are best, since they are compatible with most flowers. Felt can be used for Christmas plaques or special colour bases. Teapot stands, or trivets, can also serve the purpose, and the small round ones with legs can be painted black to resemble Japanese bases.

There is a kind of compressed cardboard available at some do-it-yourself shops. This is an excellent material for making bases, as it is about ½ in (1.3 cm) thick, lightweight and easy to cut. Unfortunately, it is usually only obtainable in large sheets, so you could team up with other flower arrangers to share the cost.

The lids of old cake tins can be covered or painted, and for Christmas designs

A wide range of vases, in different shapes, sizes and colours, will help to bring variety and interest to your designs.

you can use hardboard or chipboard covered with coloured foil. On the whole, it is better to keep your fabrics plain and matt, as highly patterned or shiny fabric will detract from your flowers.

As for colour, the beginner should stick to mossy and grass greens, browns and greys. The greens blend in with most foliage, the browns are good for dried arrangements, and neutral greys will look good with bright colours combined with grey foliage. As you become more experienced, you can link your bases to the colours of your flowers.

For interpretive arrangements, bases can be cut in irregular shapes and then painted. Boards dotted with glue and sprinkled with sand are ideal for seascapes, and wood slabs or pieces of slate are ideal for landscape arrangements. A good way to make a cheap base for a landscape arrangement is to cut out a piece of hardboard or chipboard in your

required size, using an irregular-shaped pattern (experiment with newspaper until you have something you feel is pleasing, then transfer your paper shape to the hardboard, trace it and cut it out with a hacksaw). Mix a small quantity of filler compound and slap over the shape, leaving some areas rough and some smooth. When it is dry, paint with a mixture of blackboard paint and silver paint, which will result in a pewter-grey shade that makes your base look like slate. (It is possible to buy both silver and matt-black paint in model-paint sizes, but since these are such useful colours slightly larger cans are probably cheaper).

Other items you could use for bases are small trays, breadboards, rush mats or any plain table mats. Occasionally pieces of marble or glass bases can be bought, which are useful for a change of texture in your collection. Many flower clubs sell flocked or fabric-covered bases in various sizes.

THE FOUR BASIC FORMS

ACH OF THE FOUR basic forms described here provides a simple geometric structure on which a flower arrangement can be built. The materials you have at hand and where you decide to place your arrangement will determine the form you choose to work from.

The history of flower arranging dates back to ancient times and all kinds of patterns and forms have evolved through the ages, mainly under the influence of the West and the Far East. The Japanese, for example, have practised the art for well over a thousand years, and they are renowned for their pure classic asymmetrical designs. Books, paintings and mosaics are a valuable historic record – there are the Byzantine floral mosaics in Ravenna with their tall symmetrical designs, the stylized Dutch and Flemish flower paintings of the seventeenth and eighteenth centuries, and the proliferation of books and magazines on the art of flower arranging in Victorian times. Definite rules of arrangement, however, were established during this century.

Horizontal arrangement (ABOVE) of pink carnations, pink bud tulips and gypsophila. One more tulip is needed on the left to complete the symmetrical form.

Vertical design (TOP RIGHT) of tall blue iris and yellow double gerbera. To keep their upright form, the gerberas are supported with an inner wire.

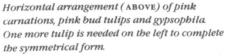
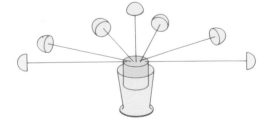
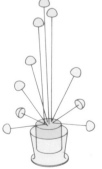

ABOVE LEFT *Symmetrical five-point design with spray chrysanthemums. Some of these are the spidery or rayonnante type, which provide a variation in form and tint.*

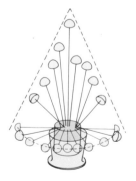

ABOVE RIGHT *Asymmetrical design of tulips and spray carnations. The flowers have been carefully graded in size towards the centre.*

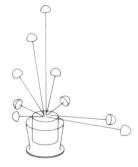

HORIZONTAL ARRANGEMENTS

ARRANGEMENTS WITH A horizontal emphasis are particularly suitable for table centrepieces where the design should not be so high and bushy that it acts as a hedge between the diners. It is also an excellent style for 'window-dressing' an empty fireplace in summer, or a mantelshelf, particularly in a fairly small room where a tall design might otherwise be overpowering.

While too many rigid rules and regulations applied to what is not only a technical skill but also an art form can be stultifying to progress, some of the most obvious rules do make sense. For example, most basket shapes would suggest a horizontal arrangement and that the handle should be left free from encompassing foliage so that it is easy to hold. On the other hand, there may be instances where the designer might feel it necessary to place a few tall flowers above the handle. However, in order to

ABOVE *Carnations, with a frosting of gypsophila. The tulips were added last to give variation of colour, shape and texture.*

BELOW *A subtle horizontal design from Korea, composed of pink dahlias, yellow roses and white antirrhinums enlivened with variegated foliage.*

MAKING A
HORIZONTAL DESIGN

1 To make a horizontal design, first decide on the colour and texture of your design and gather your materials together. Here the yellow and orange of the flowers pick up the colouring of the foliage at the centre. 2 Cut well-soaked floral foam so that it fits the container you have chosen. 3 Not every design need be constructed from the outside inwards. Begin in the middle of this design, masking the foam with foliage and roughly describing the shape intended. 4 Now insert your line flowers. 5 (OVERLEAF).

5

break the rules, one must first learn to apply them. To avoid frustration and disappointment, it is better to stick to basics until you feel your designing is becoming more fluid.

Sometimes a flower arranger is invited to place flowers on the church altar, though in some churches this is not allowed. A horizontal design is usually the most suitable and should be kept symmetrical to balance the existing symmetry, and often the simplicity of other appointments nearby. Having

completed the design, always go to the back of the church to check that the central flower is not taller than the cross, which is either on or just behind the altar. It is usual when making a horizontal arrangement to establish the spread of the design first. Fix these two lines first and then decide the height and the depth and work within this framework.

Arrangements for the dining table whether at home or at a banquet are usually horizontal otherwise no one would be able to see or be seen. The

5 Strengthen the lines with the addition of more flowers, being careful not to overcrowd the arrangement.

maximum width of such designs is crucial, for there must be ample space for the guests to eat or, in the case of a banquet, speakers notes and microphones. Graceful and near-symmetrical horizontal designs, sometimes joined with ribbons or ropes of green foliage can effectively enhance what might otherwise be a rather stark dining table.

VERTICAL ARRANGEMENTS

A SIMPLE DESCRIPTION of vertical is that the line is at right angles to the horizon. If one then translates horizon into container-rim, it will give a good idea of how material should be set in place.

First establish whether the arrangement is to be a facing design – that is viewed from the front only – or an all-round design. This affects the position of the first main stem. For a facing design, the main line must be set in towards the back of the foam, and for an all-round arrangement, it should be set in the centre of the foam.

The main line should be straight and definitive, and establish the maximum height of the arrangement. Then, two or three more lines should be inserted very close to the first one and parallel to it, each one slightly shorter than the previous one. These will emphasize the main line and help to make it visually stronger.

The next decision is to determine the maximum width of the design. For a facing arrangement, insert two lateral stems aiming towards the position where the main line was inserted.

For an all-round design, insert five stems of equal length radiating from the central line.

All that remains to be done is to add further material at intervals, keeping within your established framework.

Strong vertical arrangements of purple irises softened by downward curving stems of yellow forsythia (RIGHT) and a charming combination of freesias with chrysanthemums (OVERLEAF). Notice the interesting positions of the flower heads and the way in which profile and full views combine to make a flowering composition.

Straight-stemmed flowers like gerbera are particularly suited to vertical designs. The gerbera may curve, but wiring will ensure that the flower remains upright.

1 To wire a flower insert a piece of wire of the correct thickness downwards through the centre of the flower stem into the middle of the flower head.

2 Press the wire gently but firmly back into the centre of the flower with the blade of your knife. Care is needed to ensure the flower remains undamaged.

A well balanced vertical arrangement. The unimaginative use of four allium (detail) is clearly in need of a little support material. Adding deep red spray carnations and foliage in a design on two levels makes a far more interesting and dramatic use of the allium.

SYMMETRICAL ARRANGEMENTS

THIS IS THE PUREST FORM of all design. Perfect symmetry or visual balance is present in classical architecture, sculpture, tapestries, medieval paintings and containers, yet few of us are consciously aware of it. Even the word itself suggests grace and elegance.

The technical definition, however, is far more mundane: that the object should be divided into two parts, both being equal in content. Translated into terms of flower arranging, this does not mean that all designs have to be facing. They can be circular, oval, horizontal or vertical, as long as they can be equally divided. Thus, a design with vertical emphasis may also be symmetrical, or the reverse, for it might quite possibly be asymmetrical and still be vertical.

As few flowers are identical, it is not easy to achieve perfect symmetry with living material. Therefore, an arranger is not expected to measure the two sections exactly for height, width and depth. Your design should rather appear to be symmetrical giving a satisfying visual balance, bearing in mind, of course, that the basic disciplines should be respected. If your lines are well-placed and the materials carefully chosen, then successful results should follow. A simple arrangement can be made by placing an even number of stems at either side of the central stem.

In choosing the material it is probably easier to get a satisfactory result if you use not more than three types of flower,

Strong, clear lines are first established for this beautiful symmetrical arrangement of yellow double freesias, darker yellow spray chrysanthemums and purple liatris, with interesting dark green foliage, to emphasize the yellow blooms.

For this arrangement the base is first masked with green hellebore (ABOVE, LEFT) before the three main lines are set in place (ABOVE).

Notice (RIGHT) how the third flower down to the right of centre has been placed so as to avoid too formal an effect.

that is, flowers of differing shapes and sizes, such as delphiniums, roses and spray chrysanthemums. Apart from the type of flower and colour, the classic 'recipe' includes line flowers, which are the materials that give gradation, normally with buds and semi-open flowers, plus materials for emphasis. These are usually mature blooms, often of a strong, clear colour and shape.

Your choice of colour will naturally play an important role in determining symmetry. You may, in fact, make a design which is entirely symmetrical from the point of view of line, yet if the colour values are off-balance, it will never appear to be symmetrical. Do not let this deter you from making symmetrical arrangements for table centrepieces and display. The style cannot possibly be mastered in one easy lesson, so keep trying out different types of materials during each season of the year. Remember that it is better to begin with a simple design and graduate to more complicated ones as you gain confidence.

ASYMMETRICAL ARRANGEMENTS

THIS FORM OF DESIGN is the reverse of the symmetrical type – which is, that each side should be different, possibly in content and certainly from the point of view of line and emphasis.

However, as with the other forms, it needs a firm framework on which to build. So, although the main line may not necessarily be set into the middle of the arrangement, it must be seen to be the main line that runs straight into the centre of the design.

Asymmetrical arrangements can also be set vertically or horizontally, but care should be taken so that they are not confused with free-style designs.

BELOW *Vertical emphasis. Tulips and spray carnations in an elegant vase.*

However, try not to become intimidated by too many definitions, rules and regulations. These few pointers are intended to help and not to confuse. When you are making an arrangement, imagine, in essence, that the framework is made up of bare twigs which you will then 'dress' with flowers and foliage. Keep the basic structure simple and well-defined to ensure a successful arrangement.

White jug and flowers in the first stages of preparation (FAR LEFT, TOP). Foam is wedged into the neck and the main lines are set in place. Notice the small but very definite bud carnations describing the structure.

At the next stage (LEFT, TOP), existing lines are strengthened with more flowers, and some foliage is inserted. The main lines are now to some extent masked.

LEFT, BOTTOM Pink carnations alone would be rather bland, so a little red alstroemeria is added. Notice how the main structure is kept, while at the same time flowers and foliage is added.

A strong structure described with lemon antirrhinums (RIGHT), which is repeated at varying lengths. Brown spray chrysanthemums at the heart of the design provide variation in colour and form. A mixed arrangement of freesia, spiced with a few stems of tolmiea and strengthened at the heart with alchemilla foliage (DETAIL).

CHAPTER 2:
TRADITIONAL
FLOWER ARRANGING

P EOPLE HAVE ARRANGED *flowers to produce*
beautiful and even spectacular effects for
centuries. There is a special joy in taking already
pretty objects and grouping them together to form
an image that gives pleasure to others. In this
chapter we show how to make your own flower
arrangments in a series of simple step-by-step
guides. Then we illustrate some more unusual
arrangements suitable for special occasions.

STEP-BY-STEP ARRANGEMENTS

GREEN AND WHITE

MATERIALS

Green cherub container filled with soaked floral foam, green base. Spray carnations, carnations, philadelphus (mock orange), *Tellima grandiflora* and its foliage.

1   Make a diagonal line with the spray carnations.

2   Place heavy carnations toward the middle of the arrangement.

3   Fill in with mock orange and tellima foliage, bringing some over the rim of the container.

4   Place the arrangement on the base.

FIVE CARNATIONS

MATERIALS

Container with two openings, pinholder, base. Yucca leaves, plantain stalks, carnations, fatsia leaf.

1   Add water to the container.

2   Insert the yucca leaves, cut to different lengths, at the back of the pinholder.

3   Make triangles out of the plantain stalks, and add them below the yucca leaves, bringing one of the stalks out to the side.

4   Place the carnations in position, putting one in the small opening at the side, next to the plaintain triangle.

5   Add the fatsia leaf to the opposite side.

6   Place the design on the base.

OPEN-CRESCENT ARRANGEMENT

MATERIALS

Dolphin container with soaked floral foam, oval base. Scotch broom, Spanish broom (*Spartium junceum*), chrysanthemums, privet. (If no broom is available, look for any plant material with a natural curve.)

1 Place the curved Scotch broom in the container, forming a crescent (broom is bent by putting it on top of your thumbs and gently pressing down).

2 Add the chrysanthemums, placing the smaller flowers at the ends and bringing the heavier blooms toward the middle.

3 Following the line, add the Spanish broom; fill in the gaps with the privet.

4 Place the container on the base.

TULIP IN A TANKARD

I wanted to use the last of the laburnum for this arrangement. The yellow spring flower has such lovely flowing lines, but, because of its floppy nature, it is not the easiest flower to use.

MATERIALS

Tankard with tin-can lining filled with soaked floral foam. Laburnum, tulips.

1 Insert the laburnum so that it flows well over the rim of the tankard.

2 Use a tulip at the top of the arrangement, and continue using tulips to form a diagonal line.

3 Fill in the arrangement with the laburnum and its foliage, and the tulips and their leaves. No base is required.

A longer piece of laburnum at the top would have improved this arrangement by providing a little more colour between the tulips.

ALL-GREEN ARRANGEMENT

MATERIALS

Cherub container, soaked floral foam, green base. *Alchemilla mollis,* cupressus (cypress), chrysanthemums, muscari seedheads, *Helleborus foetidus.*

1   Place the *Alchemilla mollis* and the cupressus in a diagonal line for the framework.

2   Add buds of the chrysanthemum at the top and bottom, bringing them through the design so that the heavy flowers are toward the centre.

3   Fill in with the cupressus, the muscari seedheads, the hellebore and the *Alchemilla mollis.*

4   Stand on a green base.

FRESH WITH DRIED

MATERIALS

Cherub container with soaked floral foam, base. Preserved dock and foxglove seedheads, laurel, yew, choisya, *Grevillea robusta,* beech, chrysanthemums.

1   Insert dock and foxgloves at the back of the container.

2   Bring other materials forward to create a triangular line, placing the heavier leaves nearer to the centre.

3   Add a bud chrysanthemum way at the back. Add the remaining chrysanthemums following the line of the foliage, using the heavy blooms at the focal point.

4   Stand the arrangement on the base.

SPRING MIXTURE

I very much wanted to illustrate a spring flower arrangement in this book, but the season had passed and it was early summer, so I was very lucky to get some late tulips. With a few wallflowers and a late-flowering species of lilac, I had just about enough to make this seasonal arrangement.

When making this spring arrangement, it would be better to have a little more material – three more tulips would have greatly improved the design.

MATERIALS

Container (Italian cherub), soaked floral foam taped to container. Lilac, tulips, wallflowers (Cheiranthus species, or gillyflower).

1 Place the lilac to give the design a triangular framework, bringing it forward over the rim of the container and at the sides.

2 Add the tulips, following the line, and then fill in with the wallflowers. Use tulip leaves to help fill in the gaps.

MODERN CHRYSANTHEMUM ARRANGEMENT

This arrangement is mainly for those who like to experiment with plant material. If you have no long plantain stalks, try reeds, which work equally well. You can create your own pattern by varying the angles.

MATERIALS

Three-opening container filled with soaked floral foam, tile, fabric base. Iris leaves, plantain stalks, chrysanthemums, hosta leaves.

1 Insert an iris leaf into each of the three openings, cutting the lowest one short.

2 Bend the plantain stalks into angles; place one in the tallest opening, and two in each of the others.

3 Add two small chrysanthemums to the top opening, one into the middle and two heavier blooms into the lower opening.

4 Add one hosta leaf at the side of the middle opening and one similarly at the lower opening.

5 Place on the two bases.

MAUVE MIXTURE

All the flowers in this arrangement are mauve, pink, reddish-mauve or purple, which make for an attractive colour blend.

MATERIALS

Bowl, soaked floral foam, two bases. liatris, irises, aquilegia (columbine), sage flowers, double and single stocks.

1 Place the liatris at the top of the design.

2 Add the irises and aquilegia, then continue the line with sage, aquilegia and single stocks to establish the slender triangle.

3 Insert the heavier double stocks at the centre of the arrangement.

4 Place on mauve bases, or use a single base if preferred.

PINK MIXTURE

All the flowers in this arrangement range from pink through to pinky-red. Some are from the garden and some from the florist.

MATERIALS

Marble vase, with soaked floral foam-filled candle cup placed on top. Euonymus, stocks, Japanese honeysuckle, alstroemeria, sweet williams, pink cornflowers, lilac, spray carnations, carnations.

1 Insert some of the smaller pieces of the plant material, bringing some over the front.

2 Add alstroemeria, sweet williams and cornflowers to make a triangular outline.

3 Put in some heavier flowers, and add foliage at the back.

4 Place the carnations, running them through the centre, and then fill in with the smaller flowers.

5 Set the arrangement on the base.

BERRIES AND ROSES

This design makes the most of a beautiful bunch of florist's roses by adding berries, foliage and seedheads to enhance the design.

MATERIALS

Tin can with soaked floral-foam filling, base. Privet foliage (*Ligustrum ovalifolium*), hosta leaves, muscari seedheads, *Mahonia japonica* berries, *Alchemilla mollis,* roses.

1   Make a diagonal line of privet, and add hosta leaves at the front.

2   Add seedheads, berries and *Alchemilla mollis* to the framework, keeping the berries lower in the arrangement.

3   Add the roses, keeping the buds to the top and the sides and the opened roses toward the centre.

4   Place the design to one side of the base.

ALSTROEMERIA AND ROSES

MATERIALS

Bronze cherub filled with soaked floral foam, base. Alstroemeria, *Alchemilla mollis,* roses with their leaves.

1   Place the container on the base.

2   Make an outline out of the alstroemeria, carrying some over the front.

3   Add the *Alchemilla mollis,* following the line.

4   Add the roses, saving the heaviest flowers for the area near the centre.

5   Add the rose leaves to fill in any gaps, and to hide the mechanics.

PINK MONOCHROMATIC

This is a monochromatic colour scheme in tints, tones and shades of red. The close-up shows the design without base and drape, still looking quite effective.

MATERIALS

Bottle, stick and modelling clay; pink drape; bottle filled with water tinted red by food colouring; candle cup, filled with soaked floral foam and taped on top; bulldog clip. Copper beech, spray carnations, roses, heuchera, escallonia.

1   Put the stick into the bottle, securing it at the neck with the clay.

2   Toss the drape over the bottle, forming a triangular shape, and secure it with a bulldog clip at the back.

3   Add the red base.

4   Place the copper beech as a background, and then add the spray carnations at the top, sides and front.

5   Fill in with spray carnations and roses, with heavier roses nearer the centre.

6   Fill in any gaps with heuchera and escallonia.

ARRANGEMENT ON A BOTTLE

As this design takes very little material, it is economical to make; any small garden or florist's flowers are suitable.

The blue bottle is rather pale, so as an experiment I filled it with blue-coloured water; this helped to make the arrangement look more stable, as you can see from the photograph.

MATERIALS

Bottle filled with water and blue food colouring, candle cup with soaked floral foam stuck on top and taped for extra security, scarf as a base. Cornflowers, cupressus (cypress), alstroemeria.

1   Insert cornflower buds to form an inverted-crescent outline. Strengthen the outline with cupressus.

2   Add alstroemeria and cornflowers to complete the arrangement.

3   Place on the scarf, which has been teased into an oval shape.

PASTELS

Pastel colours were chosen for this design – pale blue, orange, pink and yellow – with the silver-grey foliage to keep it delicate.

MATERIALS

Glass candlestick with floral foam soaked in a small candle cup, blue-covered base. (*Note*: the candle cup was stuck and taped to the candlestick). Spray carnations, forget-me-nots, alstroemeria, *Senecio greyii*.

1 Establish the framework by using spray carnation buds, the longest on the upward side, and the shorter stems for the downward flowers.

2 Add the flowers gradually to the design, keeping within the diagonal line and to the back of the arrangement. Continue adding the flowers, keeping the slightly larger ones for the focal area.

3 Use grey foliage to fill in the gaps.

4 Place on the blue base to complete the design.

This arrangement appears slightly heavy in the centre – the back carnations should have been pushed lower down in the floral foam.

ROSES WITH FIGURINE

MATERIALS

Small tin can with soaked floral foam, two green bases, figurine. Privet (*Ligustrum ovalifolium*), cupressus (cypress), Michaelmas daisies, roses.

1 Place the container on the two-part base.

2 Insert the privet and cupressus into the can to make a triangular outline.

3 Add the Michaelmas daisies, following the line.

4 Insert the roses, buds at the top and the more opened blossoms at the base.

5 Put the figurine in place.

You will note that without the figurine, more flowers would be needed.

IN AN ENGLISH COUNTRY GARDEN

Although this arrangement does not contain all the flowers mentioned in the song 'An English Country Garden', it represents a good mixture nonetheless. Any assortment from your garden – English or any other nationality – can be used as available.

MATERIALS

Two large stones, cotton birds, slate base, tin can with soaked floral foam. Campanula (bellflower), stocks, pontilla, sweet peas, pinks, aquilegia (columbine), scabious, linaria, honeysuckle, hebe, cupressus (cypress), achillea.

1 Using the campanula, start at the top to create an asymmetrical line.

2 Add the mixed flowers to follow the line. Save the heavy flowers for the base.

3 Insert the cupressus at the back and fill in the gaps with hebe and additional cupresses.

4 Place on the base and arrange the stones at one side.

5 Add the cotton birds to complete the picture.

CURVED ARRANGEMENT IN FIGURINE

MATERIALS

Figurine with screw-on candle cup filled with soaked floral foam. Box foliage, stocks, sweet peas, spray carnations, roses, scabious. Any mixture of similar flowers can be used in this pleasing design.

1 Insert a long piece of the curved box foliage to one side, and a shorter piece at the other.

2 Place the sweet peas and spray carnations at the top, making a curved outline.

3 Fill in with the smaller flowers, adding the heavy ones in the middle.

4 Bring some flowers forward over the rim, letting them flow down.

5 Fill in the gap with short flowers and small pieces of foliage.

ALL-FOLIAGE ARRANGEMENT

This arrangement uses a variety of foliage chosen for both their colour and their texture. As you can see, they make quite a colourful arrangement.

MATERIALS

Cherub with soaked floral-foam base. Privet, euonymus, oak, griselinia, acuba, aquilegia (columbine), cupressus (cypress), rue *Senecio greyii*.

1 The first placement of privet goes to one side of the arrangement.
2 Add the green and white euonymus at the opposite side.
3 Add foliage to keep the asymmetrical line, with the heaviest and most colourful leaves placed near the middle of the arrangement, thereby creating a focal point.
4 Place the arrangement on the base.

PINK FLOWERS WITH GLASS

This design consists of a mixture of pink-toned flowers, most of which came from the garden. Colour linking is also a good way of enhancing florist's flowers. The glass helped to add a different texture.

MATERIALS

Bottle with stick secured inside with modelling clay, pink drape, small tin can with soaked floral foam, two glass stands, glass base, glass baubles. Lilies, *Dicentra formosa*, cornflowers, scabious, stocks, sweet peas, sweet williams, spray carnations.

1 Arrange the drape in a triangular shape over the stick-filled bottle.
2 Put the glass base on to the stands, and the tin can on one side of the base.
3 Make a framework, starting with the tallest flower following the line of the drape.
4 Add the flowers to fill the centre, top and sides.
5 Place the heavy flowers in the middle, and fill in with short-stemmed flowers to hide the mechanics.

TWO-TIER FOLIAGE ARRANGEMENT

MATERIALS

Wrought-iron container filled with two small tin cans containing soaked floral foam, green base. Assorted foliage, including berberis, weigela, lonicera, privet, cupressus (cypress), rue, euonymus.

1 For the top of the arrangement, use curving pieces of the plant material, following the line of the container.

2 Add small snippets of foliage, working in various colours and textures as you go. Add the brightest colours at the centre.

3 For the lower part, make a horizontal line with the lonicera, and add small pieces to fill in, using the most vivid hues at the front.

4 Place the finished design on the green base.

ORCHIDS, FERNS AND FIGURINE

The ferns were 'lifted' from a potted plant for this design. As it was a fairly substantial fern, I was able to take quite a few without injuring the plant.

MATERIALS

Base, painted tin can, soaked floral foam, figurine. Iris leaves, ivy, nephrolepsis ferns, orchids.

1 Place the container on the base. Insert the iris leaves at the back and the ivy at the bottom, bringing some over to cover the can.

2 Add the ferns to give an asymmetrical line.

3 Place the orchid sprays so that they run through the design, bringing some forward to the front of the arrangement.

4 Set the figurine to one side of the arrangement to complete the picture.

HORIZONTAL DESIGN

This small design is suitable for the top of a bookcase or a coffee table. It could also be used as a table decoration.

MATERIALS

Painted tin can filled with soaked floral foam, oval base. Roses, spray carnations, *Alchemilla mollis*.

1 Begin with the rosebuds to form a low outline.

2 Add the carnations and *Alchemilla mollis*.

3 Bring the fuller flowers toward the centre.

4 Fillin the gaps with alchemilla and its foliage, along with a few more leaves.

5 Place on the base.

THE DANCER

Any garden flowers, such as sweet peas or side shoots of larkspur, would look attractive in this type of arrangement.

MATERIALS

Figurine container filled with soaked floral foam. Weigela, spray carnations, roses.

1 Insert the weigela to form an arch over the figurine.
2 Add the spray carnations to the sides.
3 Place the roses so that they are running through the design.
4 Fill in with spray carnations, rose leaves and short pieces of weigela to hide the mechanics.

FLOWERS FOR SPECIAL OCCASIONS

HALF THE FUN of arranging flowers is to make a design to celebrate a special occasion, and this is when the flower arranger's creativity is put to the real test and when it will be most admired.

The information given on the following pages explains how to make wedding bouquets, head-dresses and posies and how to wrap a gift bouquet. Also included are ideas for the most appropriate flower designs for weddings and christenings and for church decoration.

A tiny baskette or bascade (RIGHT) which is, in effect, two large corsages with very long handles which are covered with ribbon and joined firmly together at the centre.

BELOW A classic style bouquet composed of seven orange gerbera, each of them supported by an internal wire. Five bergenia leaves underline the cental point, and three gerbera 'stems' have been added to create an impression of a semi-natural group.

WEDDING BOUQUETS AND POSIES

All brides deserve lovely flowers for their special day. But never be confused by the vast choice of style and colour, for, while the materials will vary considerably from season to season, the basic shapes remain constant. First of all, decide what type of bouquet you would like, and, if possible, plan the colour and shape of the bridesmaids' flowers and any table decorations at the same time. In this way, all the wedding floral decorations will harmonize. Originally, all bouquets were loose, natural bunches or tightly-packed nosegays simply tied and held in the hand. In the late eighteenth and early nineteenth centuries, they became very large and very heavy. Presumably this was in line with the upsurge of interest in horticulture at the time when many more foliages were available and some brides were almost submerged by cascades of ferns.

However, in the early 1950s, bouquets began to diminish in size and the technique of making them became far more precise and delicate. Many were miniature works of art. Professional designers were able to do this type of work because they had access to better materials. Some of these materials include such things as finer wires, different coloured binding tape and ribbons in a multitude of colours, widths and designs.

Even so, the basic form was much the same. That is, flowers on single stems or taped 'stems' were built into a simple design that could comfortably be held in one hand.

A classic shower or waterfall shape is still very popular with brides; smaller designs for the bridesmaids. It is adaptable to almost any type of flower, is easy to hold and looks elegant.

The semi-crescent design is an extremely graceful bouquet. It is just as effective with simple flowers on their natural stems as with 'special wedding' flowers which have to be wired into trails.

The full-crescent is another popular and lovely variation, particularly suitable to accompany brides with long, full-skirted gowns.

Whether the bouquet has ribbon trails or not, it should always be neatly finished at the back with a small bow and a comfortable ribbon handle.

The bridal bouquet will, of course, be lovely, the bridesmaids and flower girls complete the wedding picture. Happily, whatever the time of year, there is a wide selection of flowers and designs for them to choose from.

Bascades resemble baskets of flowers (although they are actually designed like small bouquets with a ribboned handle), and they can be copied in any size to suit both child attendants and taller bridesmaids. A head-dress to match, in either real or fabric flowers, completes the effect.

Pomanders (floral balls) can also be designed in several sizes. The ribbon handle is, of course, graded in length according to the height of the bridesmaid. Both these and the bascades are popular with the younger attendants as they can

The classic style, unashamedly expensive when made up in lily-of-the-valley, stephanotis and white roses. These are all traditional bridal flowers, but there is no reason why the same shape should not be copied in many other flowers.

To wire and tape a hollow-stemmed flower, first cut your stem to the required length and then carefully insert a piece of wire through the stem and centre of the flower.

Using florist's tape and starting about ¹/₂ in (15 mm) up the stem, bind both the stem and wire together and continue binding until they are covered.

All the flowers are on their natural stems in this hand posy so that it can be placed in water. To make the posy, take three strips of tulle, one shorter than the other two, and gather them on wire to form circles. Place a few flowers inside the smallest frill and pull the wire tight (though not so tight that the stems break). Then, randomly position flowers around it, gather the second frill around the bunch and pull the wire tight. Position the remaining flowers followed by the third frill. Pull this last wire tight and add ribbon trimming.

A full-crescent bouquet of spray chrysanthemums, underlined with gold braid loops of varying sizes. The flowers have conveniently hollow stems so that a fine supporting wire can be inserted without damaging the flower.

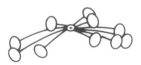

be swung around without damaging the flowers! Sometimes a wedding ceremony can prove a bit overwhelming for young bridesmaids but hand-held flowers can at least be a distraction.

For a country wedding, pomanders made with wild flowers such as marguerites (moon daisies) would look absolutely enchanting. Or maybe the bridesmaids would prefer to carry natural posies of mixed flowers. If the flowers seem limp after the wedding immerse the bouquet completely in cold water overnight. They will, no doubt, revive and last for several more days acting as a reminder of the happy day.

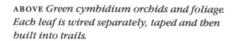

ABOVE *A sandalwood fan decorated with a small corsage of green Singapore orchids.* BELOW *A floral pomander made of tiny tulle bows decorated with a fresh flower spray.*

ABOVE *Green cymbidium orchids and foliage. Each leaf is wired separately, taped and then built into trails.*

*A semi-crescent bouquet. (*RIGHT*) An all foliage bouquet can be made at any season with any type of leaf that will tolerate being carefully wired and left out of water for several hours.*

STITCHING AND WIRING IVY

Ivy is very long-lasting, so naturally it is quite popular for bridal designs. Every single leaf must be stitched with a fine silver wire and each 'stem' neatly bound with florist's tape. The tape is not only used for a neat finish, but to seal the base of the leaf or flower stem, thus keeping in any moisture and consequently helping material to last a little longer.

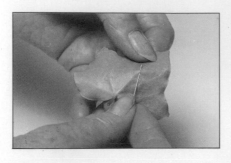  

1 *Select a sufficient number of clean, well-shaped leaves. Using a needle threaded with fine silver wire, make a small stitch at the centre back of an ivy leaf.*

2 *Carefully pull the wire thread through and, keeping the wire loop quite loose, lay one end down the side of the ivy stem and wind the other round both of them.*

3 *Next, starting at the base of the leaf, begin to bind the wire and ivy stem together with florist's tape.*

4 *Continue binding the wire 'stem' with florist's tape until your stem is the required length.*

5 *Several 'stems' of ivy can now be bound together and assembled into trails. These can be shaped to form part of your wedding bouquet.*

This classic head-dress (ABOVE) is attached to a small hair comb. You can secure it with silver wire or with clear adhesive.

Whenever possible match head-dresses with bouquets and posies. This is particularly effective with a period design as shown in the Victorian posy and head-dress (TOP RIGHT and LEFT). The bridesmaid's posy and circlet are made of fabric flowers. The circlet is secured to the hair with hair grips (bobby pins)

WEDDING HEAD-DRESSES AND PRAYER BOOK

Instead of the traditional wedding bouquet some brides prefer to carry a white bible or prayer book, with a small spray of flowers attached.

In effect, the spray follows the same kind of design as a bouquet and should be made in proportion to the size of the book. If it is too large, the whole effect is lost.

Ribbon markers are a matter for personal preference. One is usually passed through the page at the beginning of the Marriage Service and the other across the inside of the cover. These ribbons can look very attractive either left plain or decorated with tiny fresh flower heads.

For a summer country wedding, flower-decorated parasols would make charming accessories for the bridesmaids. They are quite lightweight to carry and can be closed for the ceremony. This should have no effect on the flower trimming providing it is done carefully. It is, of course, advisable to let your florist know that you would like the parasol to be used both open and closed and then the trimming can be arranged accordingly.

There is a fairly wide range of bridal parasols (LEFT) to choose from, and trimmings can be simple or elaborate. White is ideal for a prayer book spray (TOP) and different flowers made an interesting contrast. Anchor the spray firmly *to the prayer book (ABOVE) so that it fits closely to the cover.*

OPPOSITE *Fresh flowers wired on a ring make a pretty design for a family service in church.*

Horizontal-style flower arrangement for the wedding car (BELOW) built on an 'auto-corso' base.

The auto-corso has a suction base (ABOVE LEFT) on which soaked foam is secured (ABOVE).

WEDDING CAKE DECORATION AND CAR BOUQUET

If possible, the bridal cake top should match, or at least blend with, some of the flowers in the bridal bouquet. If the bouquet is made with large flowers, such as red roses, then obviously this is not feasible, but sometimes a flower can be diminished by using just a few petals and joining them in small trails as mini-flowers.

You could even place a favourite vase on top of the cake and create a design on natural stems if the flowers are suitable. The cake top design should be kept as delicate as possible and in proportion to the size and height of the cake.

Decorating the bridal car can also con-tribute to the festivity of the occasion. A suction base called an auto-corso can be arranged in exactly the same manner as a horizontal-style flower arrangement. There can be no damage to coachwork as the base is rubber. The decoration can be fixed either to one wing, or to the bonnet, attached to water-resistant ribbons stretched from either side of the windshield. Decidedly a fun addition to the bridal flowers.

The cake top (BELOW) is designed to match the all-white classic bouquet on page 60. Built in accordance with the five-point motif, all the wire 'stems' are bound at one point and then bound together to form one stem that neatly fits into the silver vase.

A two-tier cake with a small top decoration in fabric freesias and tiny daffodils, further emphasized by trailing ribbons and bows held at the four corners of the base. The detail of the decoration (ABOVE) shows ribbon bows with a single daffodil simply arranged at each corner.

FLOWERS FOR CHRISTENINGS

A christening is yet another happy occasion made more festive with plenty of flowers. What better first gift could a child have than to be surrounded by loving family and flowers?

As well as a pedestal design – or several if the church is large enough – you could have ceremonial brass candlestands which look lovely when specially dressed.

Use long-lasting flowers, if possible, rather than delicate varieties, and make sure your foam is well soaked because sometimes it is not practical to fix a container to the stand. There is generally a small rim around the candle, presumably to catch the wax, but it is sometimes possible to fit pieces of floral foam to both sides of the candle. It is advisable to seek permission from whoever is in charge before doing this, however.

Nowadays christenings are conducted within the framework of a church service, not as isolated services. This means, of course, that not only the immediate family but everyone else can enjoy the extra special flower decorations.

Do try to check them a day or so afterwards; nothing looks worse than special arrangements that are fading. No doubt the pedestals and vase designs will last, but try to ensure that everything else is cleaned up and tidied away as soon as it is past its best.

1 *To decorate a cradle (available from the florist in a choice of pink, blue or white), fix a flat disc of soaked floral foam to a prong set in the cradle. A second round of foam will be needed*

to achieve the right height, which should be impaled on the first one with fine cane.
2 *Define the basic shape with white ixia and cream alstoemeria. Insert the stems laterally.*
3 *Add five stems of freesia and a pink ribbon to finish.*

ABOVE *White longiflorum lilies, white spray single chrysanthemums and some shapely sprays of white broom dress the Christening candle. Add a white ribbon for this very special occasion.*

ABOVE *For a more special and festive effect gypsophila may be added. This is the same arrangement with a lavish quantity added.*

A simple three-point design with long-stemmed, yellow and white lilies (LEFT). Delicate, drooping yellow fronds fill the central area.

CHURCH DECORATION

It is quite a responsibility as well as a pleasure to arrange flowers for a particular church festival.

After the weeks of Lent with no flowers at all, the church can be decorated for Easter as lavishly as time, material and money will permit. Daffodils are usually in abundance together with the new foliage.

Lilies are the traditional Easter flower and some churches prefer arums. These certainly are beautiful but are not easy to arrange because of their broad stems. Fortunately, though, they are entirely tolerant of being arranged in foam, providing it is possible to add more water to the container every alternate day or so.

The longiflorum and regale varieties have thinner, more woody stems and are much easier to arrange. They last just as well and also tolerate being arranged in foam providing the water level can be checked from time to time. These lilies are usually transported when they are very young, before the flowers open, to prevent them from being damaged. So buy them at least by the beginning of Easter week so that they can develop and show some bloom (as opposed to green buds) by the time you want to arrange them.

MAKING A CHURCH DECORATION

ABOVE 1 *Choose a deep bowl and fill it with foam. The second part-block is attached with adhesive tape. Use pieces of stem to prevent tape from cutting into the foam.*

ABOVE 2 *For such a large design, add a third smaller block of foam to the base, again setting stems in position to protect the foam, and securing it firmly with tape.*

ABOVE 3 *Insert the main lines of this three-point design first, well back in the foam. The side view shows these first stems in place, leaving the centre of the foam clear.*

RIGHT 4 *Add more stems, still as far back in the block as possible. See that they do not 'march forward' as this picture indicates, since this will result in a stodgy-looking effect and may upset the balance as well.*

5 *The completed design of daisies, lilies and broom. A classic example of a well proportioned design of white with a softening of yellow.*

MAKING A
GIFT BOUQUET

Bouquets wrapped in clear cellophane with bright, richly looped bows suggest glamour, success, honour and royal occasions. To add such a touch of glamour to a bouquet of flowers from your own garden or from the florist is not difficult and is worth the effort.

You will need cellophane paper, a generous length of water-resistant ribbon and a staple gun. If you can plan ahead, it is well worth having an idea of the colour combination you want in your bouquet before you choose the ribbon, and you can then either match one of your colours or perhaps pick a ribbon that makes a strong contrast. Follow the instructions (RIGHT) and you will be able to add a touch of luxury to a gift of flowers.

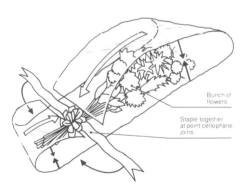

Bunch of flowers

Staple together at point cellophane joins

TOP 1 *To wrap a gift bouquet, first make sure that all stems of both flowers and foliage are clean and free from thorns or odd leaves. Then arrange the flowers and foliage as attractively as possible, longer stems to the back, keeping the shorter ones to the front. Try not to cut stems any shorter than absolutely necessary.*

ABOVE 2 *Tie the bouquet together at a comfortable tying point with a multi-loop bow of water-resistant ribbon, which has been tied across the centre with a fairly long piece of the same ribbon. It is a good idea to prepare the ribbon at the start. The bouquet should then be laid on the cellophane leaving the bottom to fold over the flower heads.*

ABOVE, LEFT 3 *Arrange the cellophane over the flowers and stems so that the ends meet at the tying point. (About twice the length is enough).*

ABOVE 4 *Then staple once each side at the tying point keeping the cross ties outside the paper.*

ABOVE 5 *Cross the ties at the back and bring around to the front, finishing off with another bow across the centre of the first bow. Staple the edges at least twice, but to prevent the inside from steaming up, be careful not to overseal.*

CHAPTER 3:
NATURAL FLOWER ARRANGING

P RODUCING FLOWER *arrangements using wild flowers and without artificial aids, using only natural ingredients, provides a stimulating challenge. It is delightful to be able to point out that your elegant design was achieved with the same things that our ancestors used many centuries ago. Considerable guidance is given on locating and conditioning wild flowers, with advice on other useful natural plant material. A series of step-by-step illustrations then helps you to make your own naturally beautiful arrangements.*

FINDING AND CONDITIONING WILD FLOWERS

SO MANY ARRANGERS are what I call 'floral snobs'; they won't use anything that has not been cultivated, and in doing so miss out on some of the most interesting plant material of all – wild plant material.

Now let me make it quite clear that you must *never* pick anything that is rare. Also, I would never cut anything that has only a small clump growing. But a lot of wild plants are so numerous that they are almost classed as weeds. For instance,

Queen Anne's lace is so prolific that it borders on the indecent, but what a lovely flower it has! It looks very delicate, but don't you believe it: I used it for a pedestal in a church flower festival, and when the festival was over it was left there and lasted for another week. Mind you, I *did* place it in water with a pinholder and wire for mechanics.

Various yarrows are interesting to use in flower arrangements, and though they are usually white, you can occasionally

find a pink variety that is rather pretty. Rosebay willow herb, or fireweed as it is often called (due to its rapid appearance on ground that has been burnt out by fire), is often found growing on waste ground. Goldenrod is another plant that pops up with great frequency, although I believe this is really a garden escapee. Also, there are various members of the daisy tribe growing wild, from the oxeye daisies to the little lawn daisies, as well as a multitude of flowers with rayed petals that are daisy-like in appearance.

A great number of these plants can be found on grass verges by the side of the road, and as most road-side grass is frequently mown, I shouldn't think you would be endangering any species by picking them. Damp places near streams often provide wild iris and arums, and you will often find meadowsweet and forget-me-nots growing in these situations. Berries, hips and interesting seed pods can often be found to use either when they are fresh or in the autumn, when they have dried on the plant.

Most wild flowers lose moisture rapidly, and it is advisable to ensure that you have some means of protecting them on the way home. Ideally a bucket of water is the best solution, but, failing that, a damp cloth or newspaper wrapped around the stems and kept as cool as possible will give them a good chance of survival. Avoid carrying them, as even the smallest amount of body heat from your hand can make them deteriorate.

A free arrangement of wood-sorrel, speedwells and buttercups in a clear glass jar. No need for foam here – the flowers are simply grouped and set in the jar to be held in place by its neck.

ABOVE *Vinca major and stitchwort in a handmade pottery vase produces a lovely, natural arrangement.*

LEFT *A free-style arrangement of wild parsley and a little pale mauve honesty in a basketware base decorated with a piece of contorted willow. A plastic container, prepared with a prong and a piece of soaked foam, is attached to the basketware base with Oasis-fix. The willow branch is attached to the foam by two wire 'legs'. The design is built up using the same technique as for more formal material, establishing one line at a time with a single type of flower.*

As soon as you arrive back home, recut the stem ends and give them a long deep drink of cold water before you arrange them.

A wild flower that I have always liked is the convulvulus, or bindweed. We used to call this 'Grannie's Nightcaps' when I was a child; and on our way to school we would place our finger and thumb beneath the flower head and say 'Grannie, Grannie, take your nightcap off', and press the large flower, which would then fall off. Unfortunately, when the flowers are out they only last a day and are very fragile. However, I wanted to arrange some once, so I picked them in tight bud, then placed them in a small block of very damp floral foam and carefully carried them home. The next day they were all open, and although it was a short-lived arrangement, it gave me great pleasure.

Foxgloves are plants I am very fond of, and it is easy to grow them in the garden. In the wild it can be found in purple-mauve and white. I prefer to use the smaller flowers or the side shoots as they are much daintier and easier to arrange. They blend in very well with other garden flowers, and the seedheads are attractive both when green or when they have been glycerined.

All of the materials that I have mentioned can add interest to your flower arranging. Try a landscape using oak as a background with beech and a few oxeye daisies and foxgloves; you will be surprised how attractive such an arrangement can look. Or in the autumn try a brass container filled with leaves changing colour and with hawthorn berries and rosehips. You will enjoy it just as much as flowers.

Many wild flowers produce attractive seedheads. You can use these in the green state, or, when they have dried, as additions to your winter flower arrangements.

TOP *The soft yellow heads of cowslips will add a bright touch to wild flower arrangements in early summer. These flowers are rare in some areas and should not be picked.*

ABOVE *A white variety of bluebell can sometimes be found growing in the wild. Occasionally, too, it can be bought at florists.*

ABOVE RIGHT *Casually arranged wildflowers in an informal container have a charm all their own.*

OTHER NATURAL PLANT MATERIAL

IT IS IMPORTANT that the flower arranger should learn the value of plant material as distinct from flowers. Although we always refer to our craft as 'flower arranging', it covers as well the use of a wide variety of plant material.

Flowers, foliage, fruit, vegetables, berries, seedheads, grasses, lichen, fungi, driftwood, gourds — all of these items can be used in flower arrangements for the home. For example, everyone buys fruit and vegetables for the home. It is not eaten all at once, so why not use the odd apple or pepper to add interest or a different texture to your arrangements?

Grasses can be gathered from the wild; so can berries, lichen, seedheads and driftwood. Even patches of waste ground or road-side verges can yield things like teazles, plantains or dock.

Berries are very colourful items. They include the almost-black elderberries, orange wild rosehips and bittersweet, and wine-red hawthorn berries, to name but a few — all these are to be found in hedge rows and are marvellous for making a few flowers go a long way.

Driftwood is so interesting that some pieces are decorative in their own right. It doesn't even have to be found on the beach, for many woods provide decoratively-shaped branches or roots when trees are being felled. A good time to hunt for wood is after high winds, when branches have been blown down. Sometimes it pays to remove the bark; this is particularly so with ivy, whose peeled fresh bark reveals smooth wood that looks as though it has been bleached by the sun.

All found wood should have as much of the loose bark removed as possible before it is taken home (this process

The wonderful hues of autumnal foliage will donate rich browns, reds and golds to a pure foliage arrangement.

eliminates insects as well). Scrape off the remaining bark and dig out any loose pieces, then give it a good scrub in hot soapy water. Paint it with an insecticide for protection against woodworm.

FOLIAGE ONLY

Foliage is lovely in its own right, and an arrangement of leaves and stems can be just as colourful and pretty as one of flowers. New arrangers tend to think of foliage only as green, but when they start to look around them there is a wealth of different shades and patterns.

Rhus and copper beech produce bronze foliage; privet and gold-heart ivy bear yellow foliage; santolina and *Stachys lanata* (or lamb's-ears) leaves are grey, and there are myriad varieties of leaves in green and white. Add to this your glycerined foliage, which gives you brown, beige and reddish-browns, and you have greatly increased the spectrum of colours available.

I have only mentioned a few of the foliages that you can find in these hues. There are more subtle tones as well, like the blue-grey of rue and of some pines. An especially colourful example is a berberis that is purple splashed with pink.

Autumn hues give us yellow, reds and oranges, and although they don't last all that long, such foliage can make a beautiful arrangement. Even if you are stuck with all green, you can still create a pleasing arrangement; the secret is to vary the shape and texture as much as possible.

When you do have a good selection of foliage, treat it as you would flowers. You can make a background with something ordinary like green privet, adding your more colourful foliage to the front of the design. Focal areas can be a bit tricky to find in foliage, so use rosettes of the most colourful leaves, or houseleek (hen-and-chickens) rosettes.

For afternoon tea in the garden, a high-profile arrangement that includes luscious, ripe strawberries speared on wooden cocktail sticks.

STEP-BY-STEP ARRANGEMENTS

1

2

3

BLOSSOM TIME

MATERIALS

Base, water-holding pinholder, florist's clay. Apple-blossom stems, cypress foliage, alstroemeria (Peruvian lillies), roses.

1 A water-holding pinholder is fixed to the wooden board with dabs of florist's clay. The apple blossom stems from an 'L' shape, with sprays of cypress softening the angle.

2 The deep pink of the two-tone alstroemeria (Peruvian lilies) echoes the stronger colour in the apple blossom petals. The rose at the base will form the focal point of the design.

3 The cluster of roses softens the severe outlines formed by the apple twigs. The fans of cypress foliage around the base complete the task of concealing the stem holder.

1

2

3

BOLD STATEMENT

MATERIALS
Vase, wire-mesh netting. Night-scented stocks, lilies, hydrangea, gerbera, irises, daffodils, gypsophila, cornflowers.

1 An amusing 1940s' vase calls for a casual floral arrangement that does not overpower the striking container. The height is set by night-scented stocks and golden lilies held in crumpled wire netting.

2 The bulbous mushroom shape of the container is complemented by large blooms: a head of blue and green hydrangea and a single orange gerbera. The lilies are clustered together to strengthen their colour impact.

3 One gnome appears to be supporting a sun-burst arrangement completed by the addition of irises, daffodils and gypsophila. The perennial cornflowers close to the rim of the vase provide a strong colour contrast.

1

2

JEWEL BOX

MATERIALS

Small, lidded wicker basket, plastic for lining, block of foam, cocktail sticks (to prop up lid). Sweet peas, lilies-of-the-valley, pinks, foliage.

1 The small lidded wicker basket is lined with plastic to make it moisture-proof. The block of foam extends above the rim so that the stems may be slanted downwards over the container.

2 Lilies-of-the-valley follow the lines of the sweet pea stems. The five coral and saffron-striped pinks are placed so that their colour is evenly distributed throughout the design.

3 Pastel pink sweet peas and border pinks fill in the design and form a colour link between the white and the coral. A few sprays of leaves add shape definition.

1

2

BREATH OF SPRING

MATERIALS

Basket, waterproof container, block of foam, plastic prong, florist's clay. Hypericum foliage, daffodils, irises.

1 A casserole dish fitted in the craggy basket holds a block of soaked foam which is almost concealed by the sprays of glossy hypericum foliage. The three irises define the height and width of the design.

2 Golden daffodils begin to fill in the design. If their stems are too soft and pliable to press into the foam it may be necessary to strengthen them by pushing in a medium-gauge stub wire.

3 The completed shape – a host of golden daffodils contrasted with a handful of golden and white irises. This arrangement would be especially suitable to stand in a hearth or room corner.

3

1

2

3

CASCADE OF LEAVES

MATERIALS

Vase, plastic saucer, cylinder of foam, florist's clay. Ornamental cabbage, rosemary leaves, poppy leaves, lamium leaves, hosta leaves, hollyhock leaves, aquilegia foliage, hypericum foliage, periwinkle foliage, fennel leaves, pampas grass leaves, ivy.

1 The saucer of foam is fixed to the vase with a band of florist's clay. Ornamental cabbage, rosemary, poppy, lamium and hosta leaves, with all their colour contrasts, begin to etch in the outlines of the arrangement.

2 Trails of ivy at the sides sweep down almost to the table top, and attractively enclose the vase. Short sprays of silver-leafed curry plant are silhouetted against the deep purple cabbage leaves.

3 The medley of foliage now includes hollyhock, aquilegia, hypericum, periwinkle and fennel, with the slim arching lines of pampas grass cascading over at each side.

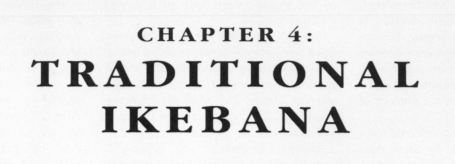

CHAPTER 4:
TRADITIONAL IKEBANA

NO BOOK ON FLOWER *arranging would be complete without a section on ikebana. Ikebana springs from a response to the beauty and infinite variety of natural plant forms, a recognition of the strength, delicacy and ephemerality of the living flowers and branches that it uses. It can be a hobby or pastime, but for many ikebana becomes an absorbing study leading to a deeper and deeper insight into an understanding of life, its contradictions and their resolution in recognition and acceptance.*

Ikebana is as varied as the people who practise it. Traditionally only natural material was used, but contemporary ikebana, responding to change, often incorporates dry material, metal, paper, cloth, glass or plastic. Some modern arrangements even use no fresh material at all.

WHAT IS IKEBANA?

THE WORD COMES from *ikiru* (to live) and *hana* (flowers and branches); thus it means 'living flowers'. Ikebana is the Japanese art of arranging flowers according to rules and principles evolved over its long history. Ikebana is also a *dō,* a path or way of self-realization. To take up ikebana is to embark on a journey of self-exploration.

Sometimes derogatively referred to as 'two sticks and a flower' by those who understand little about it, ikebana can be grand and elaborate, as in the great *rikka* arrangements that evolved in the sixteenth century. The twentieth century has, under the leadership of modern masters like Sofu Teshigahara and Houn Ohara, witnessed the development of massive *taisaku* constructed from huge tree tunks, metal, stone and plastic, the results being more akin to sculpture than to the conventional idea of a flower arrangement.

Some designs, like the classical *seika isshu-ike* arrangements made from a single material, are monochromatic and austere, others colourful and exuberant and yet others, like *chabana* (flowers arranged for the tea ceremony), simple and modest.

Anyone can learn to do ikebana: it must be approached receptively without *trying* too hard. Ikebana requires an intuitive response to the material as well as a grasp of the rules for placing the branches and flowers and, of course, the physical skills to do this securely and correctly. It is one of many techniques developed over the centuries by the Japanese for restoring their sense of *wa* or inner harmony. You begin by looking at the flowers and branches, noticing their shape, the way they grow, how they absorb or reflect light; feeling the strength and suppleness of the branches in your hands; breathing in their scent; recognizing and responding to their uniqueness so that you will be able to show this in your arrangement. You let them 'speak' to you, let the right side of the brain come into play so that you are in touch with your own – perhaps unacknowledged – creativity.

THE WAY OF FLOWERS

The original name for ikebana was *ka-dō,* the Way of Flowers. In Japan the pursuit of any art or skill, whether it be archery, martial arts or flower arrangement, is seen as a path leading to potential self-realization. Hence the names *kyu-dō,* the way of archery; *aiki-dō, ju-dō* and *kaate-dō,* the ways of martial arts; *cha-dō,* the way of tea, and so on.

In taking up any of these you have to study and master:
● the physical and technical skills required, which are called *jutsu.* (In ikebana these are the techniques for cutting, shaping and fixing the material in the correct position.)
● the theory and history, known as *gaku,* and
● the philosophy involved in the metaphysical and spiritual journey to discover who we really are. This is *dō.*

The first two can be studied and mastered in a limited time. *Dō,* however, is a life study.

Upper-class women arranging flowers (late eighteenth century). Note the attention to detail in the picture.

IKEBANA SCHOOLS

Over the centuries, many ikebana schools grew up in Kyoto. From the middle of the 18th century, they were established in the economically dynamic cities of Osaka and Edo (Tokyo) as well. While many of these schools were associated with temples, increasingly new ones were founded by gifted and enterprising arrangers who wanted to branch out on their own and develop new ideas. Among the best known of these are the *Enshū* School, the *Koryu* School, the *Misho* School and the *Kōdo* School. These were run by an *iemoto* or headmaster, who trained teachers and assistants to work under him. They graded students according to their ability and issued certificates.

In this way, ikebana grew from being the preserve of priests to becoming an aristocratic pastime, a recreation for battle-weary samurai and then a leisure interest of the merchant class. It was only in the 19th century that the term ikebana came into use to refer to the art.

ABOVE *A flower seller. The flowers in her basket are easily recognizable as flowers sold today.*

ABOVE *A Shoka Shofutai arrangement, by Senjo Ikenobo.*

EQUIPMENT

ALL TASKS ARE easier and more pleasurable with the right equipment. The tools and other items described here are especially designed for ikebana. Anyone with a serious interest in studying ikebana should consider acquiring at least a *kenzan* and *hasami*. They will prove a good investment.

Very little outlay is needed to start practising ikebana. For your first arrangement, which will be a moribana style, you will need a shallow, flat-bottomed container, preferably a dark colour, 8–12 in (20–30 cm) in diameter and about 2 in (5 cm) deep. A suitable dish can be found in most households. Then you will need something to cut with. Initially, you could get by with a combination of florist's or other scissors to cut the flowers and a pair of secateurs for the branches.

The third thing you will need is a *kenzan*, or pinholder. This is something you are less likely to have and, since it cannot be improvised it will probably be your first purchase.

KENZANS OR PINHOLDERS

A *kenzan* (from *ken*, meaning sword, and *zan*, mountain) consists of a heavy leaden base with strong, sharp steel needles to support the flowers and branches embedded in it. Pinholders for Western flower arrangements are not designed to be used with branches and are generally neither strong nor heavy enough for ikebana. A Japanese kenzan will prove the better investment.

Kenzan come in a variety of shapes and sizes, from tiny round *gokumame* (barely ½ in [1.5 cm] in diameter), for miniature arrangements or holding a single flower in a floating arrangement, to weighty *gokudaimaru*, measuring 5 in (12.5 cm) across and capable of supporting heavy branches. The most convenient shapes are round and rectangular. A quarter-circle fits snugly into the corner of a rectangular container or against the curve of a round one. Linked *kenzan*, like the poetically named *nichi-getsu* (sun and moon, a circle and crescent) *kenzan*, give three *kenzan* in one. Joined they make one large *kenzan*, separated you have two smaller ones.

Selection of Kenzan *and Shippo. From top left: shippo/kenzan; kenzan with cross of wider spaced needles; tiny round gokumame for miniature arrangements, linked sun and moon kenzan; linked rectangles with differently spaced needles; large round gokudaimaru; long, thin rectangle; quarter-circle; 3 in (7.6 cm) rectangle; sun and moon separated.*

Your first *kenzan* should be at least 3 in (7.5 cm) in diameter, otherwise it will not be heavy enough to support the material. The shape you choose should suit the container you plan to use with it. A point to consider when selecting a *kenzan* is the spacing of the needles. At first, avoid one where these spaces are either very closely or very widely spaced. The former are useful when using thin stems, like freesias and spray carnations, or soft stems, like tulips and iris; the latter are easier for fixing thick branches. You will be using a mixture of material. Some *kenzan* have a central cross of widely spaced needles with more closely spaced needles in between. This is a practical solution.

SHIPPO

Another support sometimes used for moribana arrangements consists of interlocking circles into which branches can be fitted. This is useful for heavy material, but not as easy to master as a *kenzan*. Combined *shippo/kenzan* are available.

KENZAN MATS

Small round and rectangular rubber mats that fit underneath the *kenzan* and prevent it from marking the container are recommended. You can cut your own from foam rubber, but the mats are cheap and durable.

CARE OF KENZAN

A good *kenzan* should last for years. After use scrub with a clean stiff brush, rinse and store upside-down when dry. If the needles get bent or if dirt gets caught in between the needles, use a *kenzan-naoshi*.

KENZAN-NAOSHI

This is a simple and practical tool for cleaning and repairing *kenzan*. It consists of a small, hollow brass rod with a bell attached to help you find it. The head of the rod unscrews, enabling it to be used in two ways: to straighten bent needles and to clean the *kenzan*.

ABOVE Kenzan *with* Kenzan *mats and* Kenzan Naoshi *round and rectangular mats to go underneath a* kenzan kenzan-nooshi *showing end unscrewed.*

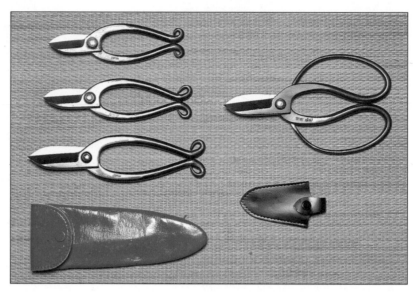

ABOVE Hasami: Tsurute & Warobi *with cose & cap. From left: three sizes of* tsurute *with* hasami *case below;* warobi *and scissor cap.*

HASAMI: IKEBANA SCISSORS

Hasami are the serious ikebana practitioner's most valuable item. Like a *sushi* chef's knife, it is their one most valued and indispensable tool.

If you are serious about ikebana, sooner or later you will want your own *hasami.* They do all the cutting you need; thick branches, thin stems, delicate leaves and petals. This well repays their initial cost. Their simplicity and elegance make them a pleasure to handle and, unless misused, they should last for years.

Two styles are available: *warabi,* which have looped handles like Western scissors, and the more widely available *tsurute* (illustrated in this book). Try out both and choose the one that suits you.

Hasami come in different sizes. Try them out, feel their weight and only then decide which feels the more comfortable in your hand.

CARE OF HASAMI

Hasami need little care. Wipe them clean and dry them after use. Rub now and then with an oily rag. Properly used they should not need sharpening, but it is possible to sharpen them on a carborundum steel. Although they will not be as good as new after sharpening, they will serve as a useful second pair.

Two words of warning: *Never* twist the blades when cutting – a sure way to blunt the edge. And never use them to cut wire. It will damage the blades irrevocably.

HASAMI CASE AND CAP

Some *hasami* came with their own case. If not, you can get a leather case or little cap to fit over the tips of the blades. This protects them from damage if dropped and also protects your pocket or the bag you carry them in, so is well worth the small outlay of money.

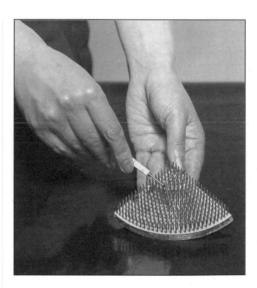

ABOVE *Bits of stem and dirt often get trapped between the needles. These should be removed or they will make the water smell. Unscrew and reverse the naoshi to expose the pin, and then use it to remove the dirt and clean in between the needles. A toothpick will also do the job fairly well.*

ABOVE *Thick branches can bend the kenzan needles. To straighten, slip the hollow end of the naoshi over the bent needle and gently pull upright. The needle should then be tapped lightly with a hammer or heavy object to secure it back in the base.*

SAWS AND KNIVES

Large saws are used for cutting branches and small saws are used for wedging, which is an advanced technique beyond the scope of this book. Like all Japanese saws, these cut as you draw the blade toward you, not on the outward stroke, as with Western saws.

The sheathed knife is used for paring the ends of branches and also for making incisions in the bark. It is not therefore regarded as being an essential purchase for beginners.

MISTER/PUMP

The combination mister/pump is used for spraying material to keep it fresh while you are working, as well as for spraying the finished arrangement. When the nozzle is removed, it can be used to pump water into stems with a high water content such as water lilies. These sometimes lose their turgidity and go limp. When the water content is restored, they stand upright again.

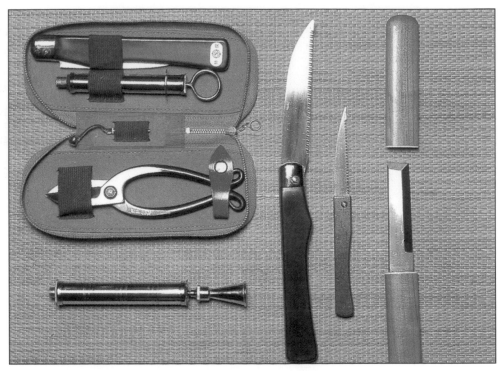

OTHER USEFUL ITEMS

Wire, raffia, rubber bands, string and gutta-percha are handy for fixing, tying, securing and shaping material. You will need a small pair of pliers and wire-cutters when using wire. Collect a supply of straight and forked sticks for making *kubari* (supports) for *nageire* arrangements. Pebbles are cometimes used to cover the kenzan, especially in those arrangements which use pond and water-side plants.

CONTAINERS

The container forms an integral part of the design of an ikebana arrangement in a way that is not always true in Western flower arrangement, in which the vase is subordinate to and sometimes completely hidden by flowers. As much care and thought goes into choosing the container, considering its sympathy with the setting, its aptness for the occasion and how well

ABOVE *From left: tool case with saw, mist sprayer,* naoshi *and* hasami; *below mister pump; large and small saws opened out; knife and wooden sheath.*

it suits the material, as into selecting the material itself. Therefore the subject needs discussion; considering formal, semiformal and informal settings.

Classical ikebana arrangements are *shin* (formal), *gyo* (semiformal) or *so* (informal). Classical containers and the materials they are made from are similarly classified.

Formal containers derive their form from classical Chinese shapes and are made of bronze, lacquer or highly glazed ceramic ware. Nowadays glass is sometimes used.

Semiformal and informal containers may be of bamboo, unglazed or matt-glazed ceramic, wood or natural objects like gourds. Baskets are popular as informal containers. In general, plain,

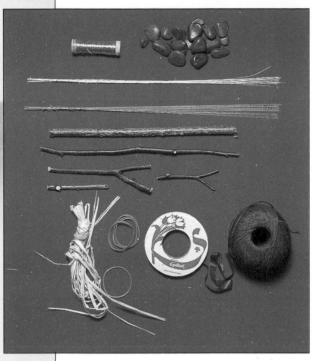

STARTING A COLLECTION OF CONTAINERS

The first container you will need is a shallow ceramic one for moribana. This should be round or rectangular, 8–12 in/ 20–30 cm across and about 2–2½ in/ 5–6.5 cm. Oval and semicircular shapes are also suitable. The container must have a flat bottom so that the *kenzan* can be placed in different positions.

The easiest colours are black, dark brown or dark blue, as all material goes with these colours, and the container it-self will then blend in with the setting you have chosen more readily. (There will be quite enough to think about without having to worry about the colour of the container.)

When you come to do *nageire* you will need a strong cylindrical ceramic vase about 10 in/25 cm tall and 3½ in/9 cm in diameter. Some *nageire* vases have a ridged or roughened band inside, below the lip. This makes it easier to fix the *kubari* and support the material. Some *kubari* exert considerable pressure on the sides of the container as the material thus balanced can be fairly heavy, so cheap machine-made ceramic vases that are liable to crack should be avoided. High-fired stoneware is a good choice as it is strong and also heavy enough to be stable. Glass is not a good choice because it shows the fixing and might crack under pressure.

Once you have been doing ikebana for a while you will no doubt want to expand your collection and look for challenging and interesting containers for freestyle

darker colours and undecorated surfaces are preferred to multicoloured, patterned ones, so that they do not compete with the material and are therefore much easier to work with.

Modern containers are another matter. There is no division into formal and informal. Instead there are *moribana* (shallow, flat-bottomed), *nageire* (tall cylindrical, square or bottle-shaped) and free-style (infinitely varied) containers. In Japan, fresh collections of containers appear each year, rather like the new season's fashion collections. Different materials like glass, metal and plastic, and fresh colours and shapes are con-stantly experimented with. Also, objects designed for one perhaps unrelated pur-pose are adapted to serve as containers for ikebana.

ABOVE *A selection of kebana containers. From left: small standing or hanging basket; bamboo cylinder for seika and* nageire *styles; square black* moribana *container, lacquered basket with handle on a* kadai; *low dish with contrasting glaze inside; antique sake bottle; small long-necked bottle.*

RIGHT *A selection of moribana containers. From left: white trough with black lines, raised on two low legs; basic round blue container; half-circle in purple plastic; large black rectangular; oval blue dish.*

ABOVE *A selection of free-style containers. From left: Funnelled log-shaped vase by Ian Auld; black compote on tall leg decorated with fine incised lines: rounded pot on three legs with streaky glaze and three openings; linked double* nagieire *vase; leaf-shaped* moribana *vase; turquoise compote with curved lip on a low base.*

ABOVE *The most basic containers: on the left one for moribana, and on the right one for nageire.*

RIGHT *A semiformal* seika *arrangement featuring a brown-lacquer* maki-ashi *base.*

and other work. Apart from containers specifically made for ikebana, interior decoration stores, antiques shops, junk stalls and flea markets may be scoured for suitable vases. You may even find yourself joining a pottery class and making your own containers. Using a container of your own design and making it is a most satisfying experience.

KADAI

A *kadai* is a base placed beneath the container both to protect the surface it stands on and to give dignity and emphasis to the arrangement. *Kadai* are more often used with classical and traditional arrangements and are obligatory with

formal styles, but may be used with modern arrangements too. The simplest is the *shiki-ita*, a regular or irregular wooden shape, polished, painted or lacquered, or an informal bamboo raft. A *maki-ashi* (bent leg style) has ends that scroll under to support it. More elaborate *kadai*, often intricately carved, may be used with *rikka* and *seika* styles. The most common colours are black, dark brown or *shu*, a warm, glowing red.

It is easy to make a simple *kadai* either from a round sliced off a seasoned log, sanded and possibly stained, or from a smooth, flat piece of wood, stained and given several coats of varnish for a durable and high-gloss finish.

SKILLS AND TECHNIQUES

IKEBANA INVOLVES THREE basic techniques. These are:
- cutting, using *hasami* and other tools
- shaping the material
- fixing the branches and flowers securely

Note: The instructions in this chapter are, on the whole, guidelines to help you achieve results rather than hard and fast rules. As you gain experience, you will find out what works best for you and no doubt you will adopt or adapt the guidelines to suit yourself, your material and your equipment.

CUTTING AND USING *HASAMI*

There are two kinds of *hasami; warabi,* and the more widely available and commonly used *tsurute,* explained in the equipment section on page 83. *Tsurute* have been used to illustrate cutting techniques in this book.

The first thing is to get used to the feel of your *hasami.* Hold them, handle them, feel their weight in your hand and practise cutting all kinds of material with them. Being familiar with scissors having looped handles, Westerners are accustomed to using the thumb in the top loop to open and the third finger in the bottom loop to close them. To open and close *hasami* you need a different action. The arm should be relaxed and free of tension all the way to the shoulder and neck. Practise this valuable movement until you find that you can do it easily and without having to think about it.

You will notice that *hasami* open and close much more freely than ordinary scissors. On examination you will find a small gap between the blades. This can be widened by placing the little finger

ABOVE *To open* hasami, *the upper handle is held between the thumb and the palm of the hand. The lower handle, allowed to drop freely, is supported by the fingers.*

ABOVE *To close the* hasami, *curl the fingers around the lower handle to raise it and bring the blades together. This makes a satisfying percussion sound.*

between the end of the handles. You do this when cutting thick branches. To narrow the gap place your forefinger between the handles. As you straighten your finger the pressure brings the blades together, and in this way, *hasami* makes it easier to cut leaves, petals and other fine material.

GENERAL TIPS ABOUT CUTTING

- When cutting, hold the part you intend to use, *not* the part you are cutting off. This eliminates the risk of its falling and getting damaged.
- Cut stems under water to avoid an airlock. This stops water reaching the leaves and flowers and they droop. Work with a bowl of water nearby for this purpose.
- The general rule is to cut stems, particularly branches, diagonally. This provides a larger surface for the absorption of water and makes fixing on to the *kenzan* easier. The exceptions are thin stems like grasses and freesias, or fleshy stems like those of daffodils and amaryllis. These are usually cut straight across.

CUTTING FLOWERS AND THIN STEMS

Flowers should be cut under water. Hold the stem above the point you want to cut, place the stem midway between the tip and the axis of the blades and cut cleanly in one movement. Until you are experienced, always cut stems slightly longer than you think you will need them. You may have to reposition them on the *kenzan* and need to recut the ends. In fact, it is a good idea to cut *all* stems a bit longer than you expect to need. Cutting is irrevocable; once a stem is too short there is little you can do about it.

CUTTING THICKER BRANCHES

Open the *hasami* to their full extent and place the branch diagonally across the mouth with the blades at an angle. Then, keeping your wrist and arm relaxed, bring the blades together. You may not be able

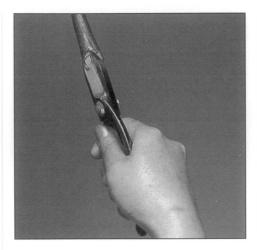

ABOVE *Hold the branch with the cut side uppermost. Split it vertically down the centre with the tips of the blades.*

ABOVE *Cutting stems under water lengthens their vase life.*

ABOVE *Cutting thicker branches: woody stems like privet, camellia or pine are more of a challenge.*

to cut right through a thick branch the first time. Open the blades, reposition the branch and repeat the action as many times as necessary.

Do not try to cut with the hand and wrist alone. The energy should come from the *hara* (the solar plexus) up through your shoulders and down your arm. To allow this energy to flow freely your back must be straight. It is often easier to cut branches standing up, feet square and firm on the ground. Do not worry if the *hasami* pinch your finger. It is one of the hazards of ikebana.

PREPARING A BRANCH FOR A *KENZAN*

Thick woody stems often need to be treated before they can be fixed securely on the *kenzan*. The most common way is to split the end. Experience will teach you which branches, among them forsythia and camellia, split easily and therefore need care. It is best to experiment with odd pieces of branch first before moving on to the real thing. Damage done during an arrangement can be time consuming to correct.

USING A SAW

Large branches may need to be sawn. Ikebana saws, like all Japanese saws, cut on the inward stroke (Western saws, on the other hand, cut on the outward thrust).

SHAPING LEAVES AND PETALS

Sometimes you need to cut away part of a damaged leaf or reshape a leaf or petal that is too large. Stiffish leaves like those of camellia present little difficulty, but delicate leaves are more of a challenge. Use your forefinger to reduce the gap between the blades to its minimum, as described on the opposite page, and cut gently and carefully with the tips of the blades. Practise on discarded leaves first.

TRIMMING

All branches and most flowers will need some trimming. Just how much depends on the material, the style, the season — summer arrangements are fuller and leafier, autumn and winter ones sparser and more austere — and your own taste. Study the arrangements in this book and notice how skilful trimming has been used to create space, reveal line and lighten and change the balance of an arrangement. Then practise on unwanted branches and flowers and notice the results.

TRIMMING FLOWERS

Generally flowers have at least two-thirds of their leaves removed. Usually these are pinched off with the fingers. Do this tidily, pinching them off at the base to leave a clean finish. Some flowers, like chrysanthemums, have a bract at the base of the leaf. These should always be removed as well. Attention to such details is the hallmark of a well-made ikebana arrangement.

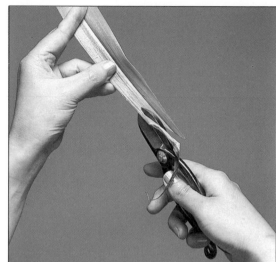
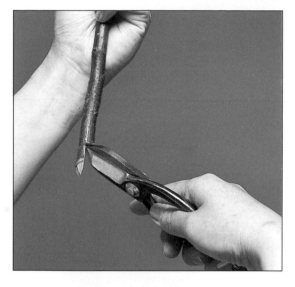

ABOVE *A very thick branch may need to be step-cut before fixing. Split the end and then cut away one side about ½ in (1.5 cm) from the bottom so that you have a manageable end that can be fixed easily and securely.*

ABOVE, CENTRE *Use tips of scissors to shape or remove damaged parts of leaves or petals.*

ABOVE, RIGHT *Cut off side branches close to the main stem.*

ABOVE *Pinching off leaves.*

TRIMMING BRANCHES

When trimming branches your aim is to clarify the line you want to use. First you need to study the branch. All branches have a front and a back, a 'sunny' (*yo*) and a 'shady' (*ur*) side. Learning to recognize this is important.

You also need to notice the movement of the branch. Branches reach upward toward the light and in ikebana all material follows this rule of upward movement. While trimming a branch, hold it as it will go in the arrangement, 'sunny' side tilted toward you and its tip reaching upward.

When you have chosen the line you want to clarify, start to cut away the side branches, checking it repeatedly as you work. Cut off side branches close to the main stem, unless you want to leave a stump for a gnarled and weathered effect. If the resulting fresh scar is conspicuous, rub it with a damp finger and darken it with dirt to blunt the rawness so that it no longer catches the eye.

Where leaves grow symmetrically, remove some to create irregular spaces on the branch. Practise on waste material and note the different effects.

ABOVE *Chrysanthemum stem before and after trimming.*

ABOVE *Scabious and love-in-a-mist before and after trimming.*

MAXIMUM USE OF MATERIAL

Where several flowers grow on one stem, as with spray chrysanthemums, spray carnations and certain lilies, a little forethought can stretch their usefulness and give you many flowers from one stem. The same is true of branches. Keep this in mind when choosing and cutting your material.

Do not throw away any material until you have finished. Flowers and side branches cut off your main stems are handy for supporting material and masking the *kenzan*. Soft thick stems, like those of chrysanthemums and lilies, are useful for 'shoes' to hold a thin stem on a *kenzan* or to prop up heavy stems. When you start making *nageire* arrangements you will need woody stems to make *kubari*, so keep the pieces of branch you cut off.

You will often find that trimmings yield enough material for a smaller arrangement and nearly always for a miniature arrangement as well. Look through trimmings with these in mind.

SHAPING YOUR MATERIAL

Sometimes you may be lucky enough to find a branch that is the perfect shape and flowers that face just the way you want them to, but there will be times you need to improve on nature. The techniques described here are not easy to grasp from a book. They need to be practised repeatedly. However, when they are mastered you will find them invaluable. Each material has its own breaking point that can only be learned from experience, so practise on waste material until you come to understand what is possible with the different materials which are available.

SHAPING BRANCHES

All branches can be shaped to bend or curve the way you want. However, some materials are more intractable than others. Choose pliable materials like yew, broom or pussy willow to start with.

Before you start, check your position. Sit or stand, back straight, feet square

ABOVE *The 'shady' back (left) and 'sunny' front (right) of cotoneaster branches.*

and your weight evenly balanced. Begin by simply holding the branch in your hands and testing its flexibility. Then decide where you want the branch to bend. Avoid the nodes (the areas where leaves, dormant buds or side branches emerge), as these are weak points.

Hold the branch in the direction you want it to go. Make sure the 'sunny' side faces you and the tip reaches up. Put your fingers under the branch so that they touch and make a 'cushion' for the branch. Your thumbs go on top, also touching. Bend gently and feel it responding.

Stop and check how you have altered the shapes. Repeat and study the result

until it is bent sufficiently. Try bending a branch to the left and another to the right. With practice your hands will start to understand the character of this material. Next time use a different kind of branch.

Sometimes you will hear a faint cracking sound as you are working. These are the fibres starting to soften and give, rather like your bones and sinews cracking when you stretch in the morning. Don't worry if you break a branch; only then can you learn how far you can go before reaching the breaking point. This not only differs for each kind of material but also depends on season and age (young and old branches, like young and old bones, break more easily).

LEFT *Privet branch before trimming.*

BELOW LEFT *The same branch trimmed to reveal the chosen line.*

THICK BRANCHES

If you want to bend a thick intransigent branch, or bend a branch at an angle rather than making it curve, make a slight cut in the bark on what is to become the outer curve. This releases the tension in the bark, and makes it easier to bend to the angle you need. This technique is particularly useful for *nageire* work.

TWISTING AND BENDING

Pliable material like yew can be twisted as well as bent to modify its direction.

ACHIEVING THE RIGHT DIRECTION

Learning how to bend a branch is one thing. Getting it to bend in the way you want is another. Study the branch carefully before you begin. Decide the shape you want to achieve and analyze how to achieve the desired effect. Understanding comes with experience. Practise the skills and study the results. After a while you will find that your hands begin to understand what to do as if by instinct.

SHAPING SOFT STEMS

Flowers require different skills and different techniques are used for *moribana* and *nageire* work. Thin branches and stems like freesias and carnations tend to snap easily. Hold the stem between the fingers, one hand near the base, the other below the head, and flex the stem gently. This makes it more pliable and can be used to induce or increase a curve.

With non-fibrous stems that have a high water content (generally monocotyledons whose leaf veins run parallel instead of branching out and forming a network) the technique is to soften the stem by gently stroking at the point at which it is to curve or bend. This technique is used with iris.

Stems of dicotyledonous plants that have a fibrous core, like chrysanthemums, hydrangeas, sweet peas and most lilies (but not arums), are gently stroked and squeezed between the fingers at the point they are to bend. This is mainly used to persuade the flowers to lean forward in a *nageire* arrangement, in which the bent stem is supported by the rim of the container. The trick is to soften the fibres just enough so that the stem will bend but retain its tension.

Great care must be taken with all these techniques, as it is very easy to break the stems.

SHAPING LEAVES

The direction of many leaves can be altered by soft stroking or lifting with the fingers. Linear leaves, like those of gladioli, montbretia and iris, are pulled upward between the fingers in one swift, firm, but gentle, twisting movement.

All leaves need to be handled with care, especially delicate leaves like those of tulips and daffodils, which rapidly lose their bloom and are all too-easily weakened if over-handled.

FLOWERS AND PETALS

A flower that is still in bud can be encouraged to open by blowing softly onto the petals. These can also be eased open very gently with the fingers. A stunning effect can be achieved with tulips in this way as seen in the floating arrangement (*ukibana*) using tulips and eucalyptus leaves, in which the flowers have been eased open to suggest water lilies.

At other times a flower, for instance a rose, may have opened too fully. Removing the outer petals will reveal the still unopened centre.

SHAPING LEAVES AND BRANCHES

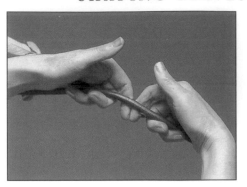

Fingers touch underneath, making a cushion for the branch.

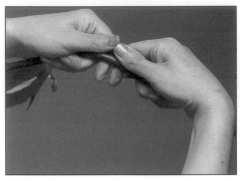

Thumbs go together on top and the energy comes from the hara up through the shoulders and down the arms.

1 *To shape aspidistra leaves: first dip the tip of the leaf into water.*

Once the tension in the bark has been released, the branch can be bent at an angle.

Nicking the branch on on what is to become the outer curve.

Bent branch resting easily in a jar.

Shaping a gladioli leaf between the fingers with a swift upward twisting movement.

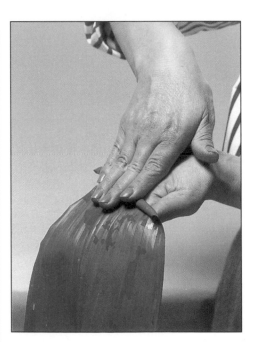

2 *Roll the leaf up tightly.*

3 Then roll it back and forth between fingers.

Hold the branch in one hand, with your thumb extended along the line of the branch.

Firmly grasp both branch and thum with the other hand, then twist and bend at the same time as if you were wringing out a wet cloth.

Encouraging a thin, spring branch to curve.

Curved springy branch in jar.

4 This will create an elegant curve.

Stroke and gently squeeze the stem at the point you want it to bend.

Bent lily with neck supported by rim of vase.

FIXING TECHNIQUES

The techniques for securing material for *moribana* differ from those involved in *nageire* work. Techniques for *nageire* are discussed in the step-by-step *nageire* section which follows on pages 118–19. Here, though, we look at how to use a *kenzan*.

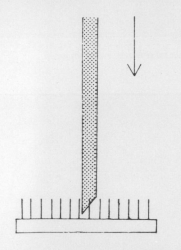

ABOVE *The branch is pushed straight down on to the kenzan with the cut side opposite the way it will lean.*

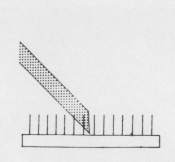

ABOVE *The branch is moved into position from the bottom.*

USING A *KENZAN* FOR *MORIBANA*:

BRANCHES

Prepare the branch by cutting the end at an angle. If it is very thick, split it or make a step-end. Hold the *kenzan* with one hand and with the other grasp the branch firmly near its base. Push the branch straight onto the *kenzan*. The angled cut faces away from the direction the branch is to lean. Make sure it is firmly fixed on the *kenzan* and then gently move it into the correct position working from the base up. Do not move it from the top as this loosens its hold on the *kenzan*.

The first time you try fixing a branch it is a good idea to put the *kenzan* on a table, where it is less likely to slip. This is also advisable when fixing thick branches that need a lot of force.

FLOWERS

Most flowers are fixed in the same way, *i.e.* pushed straight on the *kenzan* and then moved into position from the base. They need gentler handling. Soft-stemmed flowers like tulips and daffodils are cut straight; they are best fixed at the required angle to avoid handling more than is absolutely necessary.

THIN STEMS

Thin-stemmed flowers might not always be held securely by the needles of the *kenzan*. In this case, cut a piece from a thicker stem, 1 in (2.5 cm) or less in length. Chrysanthemum off-cuts are the easiest to use. Cut the thin stem at a sharp angle, slip it into the thicker 'shoe' and fix onto the *kenzan*.

Single grasses can also be fitted with a 'shoe'. If using a bunch of grass, secure the ends with an elastic band and trim before fixing.

HEAVY STEMS AND BRANCHES

You may have difficulty fixing branches and heavy-headed flowers (like gerbera or gladioli) positioned at a low angle, when they tend to collapse under their own weight. Cut a piece from a sturdy, thickish stem to fit on to the *kenzan* near the bottom of the problem stem and prop it up. Later it can be masked with foliage.

KENZAN AS COUNTERWEIGHT

When using heavy material, particularly low-angled flowers and branches in a slanting or flowing style, the weight may tip up the *kenzan*. You either need a larger and heavier *kenzan* or you can use a second *kenzan* to counterbalance the material. Turn it upside-down and fix it at the back or on the side opposite the direction of the material, so that the needles of the two *kenzan* interlock.

MASKING THE *KENZAN*

There is no need to cover the *kenzan* completely, but it should be masked sufficiently so that it does not distract from the arrangement. This is most effectively done with small pieces of foliage placed so that they reach forward on the *kenzan*. Pebbles can also be used and are especially appropriate in arrangements of waterside material. Dark pebbles are preferable to brightly coloured ones.

GETTING THE RIGHT DIRECTION

In Western flower arrangements, flowers are often placed facing straight on or looking down. In ikebana the material reaches upward toward the sun, following the line of growth. It is important to get this right as it is one of the common mistakes beginners make. Study the examples so that you learn to recognize the subtle difference between the two approaches to the material.

ABOVE *Fixing a step-cut branch.*

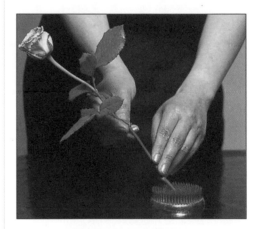

ABOVE *The stem of the rose is supported as it is moved into position.*

BELOW *Spider chrysanthemums reaching forward and upward.*

ABOVE *Thin chrysanthemum stems fitted with a 'shoe'.*

ABOVE *Heavy-headed gerbera supported with a prop. A second* kenzan *placed upside-down with the needles interlocking acts as a counterweight to prevent the weight of the flower from overtipping the* kenzan.

ABOVE *Pale gold carnation and eucalyptus stem in ikebana stem in ikebana position. Red carnation and eucalyptus in Western position.*

ABOVE *Iris reaching up in the correct ikebana position. Note the longest stem is a bud, the shortest the most open flower.*

LEFT *Full frontal and the outward and downward placement characteristic of Western arrangement.*

STEP-BY-STEP ARRANGEMENTS

GENERAL NOTES

These notes apply to the step-by-step arrangements and the variations that follow. You need to study them closely before you can truly understand the instructions for the arrangements. Mark this section so that you can find it easily if ever you need to refer back to it.

THE THREE MAIN LINES

All the basic arrangements and most of the variations use three main lines supported by supplementary material. This applies to both *moribana*

ABOVE *Showing the correct positioning of cotoneaster branches.*

and *nageire* styles. The lines are given different names by different schools but in all, the longest line symbolizes heaven (*ten*), the shortest line symbolizes earth (*chi*) and the intermediary line symbolizes man (*jin*).

To avoid confusion they are referred to as Lines, 1, 2 and 3 in this chapter and are given symbols as detailed over the page.

LEFT *Iris as they would be placed in a Western arrangement.*

LENGTH AND PROPORTION OF LINES

The length of the lines is determined by:
a. the type of material used; thin branches and smaller flowers being left longer, thick, bushy branches and bright or larger flowers sometimes cut shorter than the given measurement.
b. the main factor, *i.e.* the size of the container.

THE CONTAINER'S SIZE (C/S)

It is important to get this right, for the balance of your finished arrangement.

Measure the width and the depth of the container.

Add these two measurements to get the measurement known as the container's size (C/S). This is your guide in deciding how long to cut the material.

CHOOSING MATERIAL

For your first arrangement choose branches that are not too thick and that have clear lines. Choose flowers with strong stems and single heads so you can concentrate on the design without worrying too much about trimming and other techniques. Advice on material is given later in the chapter.

ABOVE *A sunanomono arrangement decorates a screen.*

SYMBOLS

The following symbols are used:

●
a circle for Line 1

■
a square for Line 2

▲
a triangle for Line 3

T
T for supporting material

MORIBANA BASIC UPRIGHT STYLE (LEFT-HAND VERSION)

This arrangement (see photograph over the page) brings a welcome touch of warmth. The glowing berries and golden hearts of the small chrysanthemum flowers make a cheerful combination for an autumn afternoon, when the days are starting to draw in.

Note: Instructions given for this arrangement are not repeated in the same detail for subsequent arrangements. It is assumed the reader will either internal-ize and transfer them or, if necessary, refer back to these pages.

Every style has a right- and a left-hand version. This left-hand version of the basic upright style is designed for table height to go on the left side of a table or in the left corner of a room. Adjustments may need to be made if it is placed higher or lower than table height 27–30 in (69–76 cm). First, gather your equipment and material.

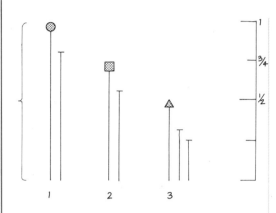

Line 1 (usually a branch) should be between one-and-a-half and two-and-a-half times the C/S depending on the character of the material.

Line 2 (the same material as Line 1) is about three-quarters as long as Line 1.

Line 3 (generally a flower) is one-half to three-quarters the length of Line 2.

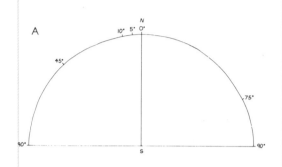

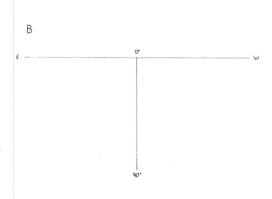

Supporting material (either flowers or branches) is shorter and less important than the line it supports. It follows the direction of the line it is supporting.

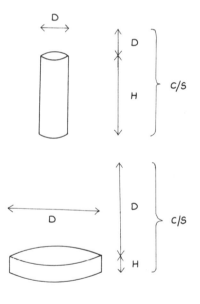

ABOVE *measuring the containers size for nageire and moribana containers.*

THE DIAGRAMS

A set of diagrams accompanies each arrangement. The top diagram shows the position of the three main lines seen from the front. It gives the angles of the lines measured to the right and left of a line 0° drawn vertically through the centre of the *kenzan*. The branch or stem may curve or bend, but the angle is measured on a line taken from its tip.

Diagram A shows the position of the three main lines seen from the front. It gives the angles of the lines measured to the right and left oa a line 0° drawn vertically through the centre of the kenzan. The branch or stem may curve or bend, but the angle is measured on a line taken from its tip.

Diagram B is a bird's eye view showing the positions of the lines forward, or occasionally backward, from a horizontal line drawn from right to left through the back of the kenzan. The measurement is taken forward or backward from this line 0°, and right or left of a central 90° line.

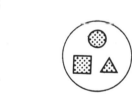

Diagram C is a close-up of the kenzan showing the point of origin of each of the three lines. Care in placing the branches and flowers correctly on the kenzan helps achieve a neat and pleasing finish.

ABOVE *Ready to start: the equipment necessary for the first* moribana *practice.*

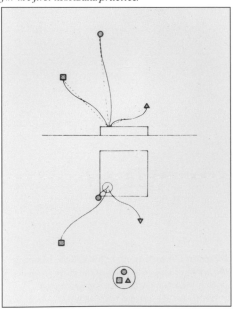

ABOVE *Diagrams showing the angles of the lines in a left-hand version of the basic upright style.*

MATERIALS

A flat-bottomed *moribana* container 8–10 in (20–25 cm) wide, a *kenzan* about 3½ in (9 cm) in diameter, *hasami* (or a pair of scissors) *and* some secateurs, a bowl of water. For Lines 1 and 2: at least two branches, two to two-and-a-half times your container's size; for Line 3 (and supporting material): three single flowers (such as carnations, roses, iris) or one or two stems of spray chrysanthemums; for masking the *kenzan:* any suitable foliage.

1 Measure your container and add its width and depth to find the container's size. Choose the longest and strongest branch for Line 1. Study the branch, decide which is the front, then measure and mark a point between one-and-a-half and two times the container's size. Hold the branch facing you with the tip pointing up and slightly leftward and cut the bottom at an angle in the bowl of water. If the branch is thick, split the end. Remove leaves and side branches to leave a clear 2 in (5 cm) at the bottom and do any preliminary trimming.

Place the *kenzan* in Position 1 (front left). With the branch still facing you check that the cut side faces right, and push it straight down between the needles of the *kenzan,* centre-back. Hold the *kenzan* with one hand to prevent it from slipping and gently ease the base of the branch left and forward until its tip is 5° to 10° left of the vertical and 5° to 10° forward. Stand back about a yard from the arrangement to check this.

2 Take your Line 2 branch, hold it upside-down against the first one and mark a point three-quarters from its tip. Now turn the branch right way up, holding it facing you with its tip pointing up and toward your left shoulder. Then cut it on the cross (under water) at the place you have marked. Remove the lower leaves and do any preliminary trimming needed.

This branch goes on the *kenzan* left-front. Push it straight down with the cut side facing right and the branch facing you. Then move it forward and to the left until the tip is about 45° left of the vertical and forward from the *kenzan.* When you stand about a yard or a metre away it should reach forward and up toward your left shoulder.

3 Choose the least open of your flowers for Line 3. Hold it upside-down to measure it against your second branch and cut it (in the bowl of water) ½ to ¾ as long. Remove the lower leaves and any others you want to. Fix this flower on the right-front of the *kenzan* and move it gently into position. The tip leans 75° to the right of the vertical and 75° forward from the *kenzan.*

Check the movement and angles of all three lines. Stand about a yard away with your work on a table in front of you. All the material should reach outward and upward toward you; Line 1 coming from the left to a point above your head; Line 2 to the top of your left

shoulder, and Line 3 to just below the top of your right arm. You should feel that *you* are the focal point of the arrangement. Do not continue until you can feel this. You will not succeed unless the movement of the lines is correct at this stage. It is best to look at the arrangement from the side to check the forward movement.

4   Add one or two flowers to support Line 3. Cut them shorter than the first flower, place them on the *kenzan* inside the triangle formed by the three main stems and ease them into position to follow the movement of the first flower. If you feel either of the branches need support add smaller branches, but be careful *not* to fill up the spaces in between the lines. This space is an integral part of the composition.

Now add small branches and foliage to mask the *kenzan.* This is more effectively achieved if you place them leaning forward. You do not need to cover the *kenzan* completely, you simply need to ensure that it is not obvious.

Tidy up so that you can view the arrangement without a distracting muddle around it. Check that the *kenzan* is still in the right position and do any final trimming.

Before adding water make sure the container is clean and free of debris.

Note: Initially it is easier to work without water in the container but, when you are more experienced, you should put a little water in the container to start with and top it up after the arrangement is placed in position.

LEFT *Used in the example: square black ceramic container with early autumn material.*
Lines 1 and 2 – Cotoneaster 'Cornubia'.
Line 3 and supporting material – small yellow-centred pompon spray chrysanthemums.
For masking the kenzan *– Arachnoides adiantiformis (leather-leaf fern) are used.*

Step 1

Steps 3 and 4

Step 2

The final arrangement.

ABOVE *Once the arrangement is complete, it is important to check the side and the bird's eye views. The final arrangement.*

BASIC SLANTING STYLE
(LEFT-HAND VERSION)

MATERIALS

Lines 1 and 2 – *Rumex acetos* (dock),
Line 3 – small white pompon bloom
chrysanthemum, for masking the *kenzan,
Alchemilla mollis* (lady's mantle), golden
privet

In this style the *kenzan* is in Position 4
(left-back).

1 Line 1 leans forward across the water
at 45° to the right.

2 Line 2 leans in the same direction at
5° to 10°. This means the tops of the two
lines are roughly on the same level.

3 Line 3 leans forward to the left 75°
from the back.

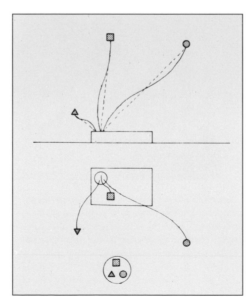

ABOVE *The completed arrangement. The
material leans forward from the back left
corner of the container and is reflected in the
water. A style for hot weather.*

The arrangement viewed from above.

Step 1 Place the kenzan *in Position 4 (left-back). Measure and cut Line 1. Fix on to the kenzan right-front and move into position leaning 45° forward and to the right.*

Step 2 Measure and cut Line 2. Fix on to kenzan centre-back and move so that the tip is 5° to 10° to the right and leaning forward. The top should be about the same height as the tip of Line 1.

Step 3 Measure and cut Line 3 and fix on to the kenzan left-front. Move so that it leans 75° left and forward. Check the three lines.

Step 4 Add supporting flowers and material to mask the kenzan. Place in position, do final trimming, check the kenzan position and, since this is a warm-weather style, top up with water to just below the brim. Check the side view (5).

MORIMONO: ARRANGEMENTS WITH FRUIT AND VEGETABLES

If you have no flowers in the house, why not try an arrangement with fruit or vegetables? This is another arrangement that can be made very quickly at the last minute using a dark shallow plate, glass dish, small grass mat or wooden bowl. The fruit and vegetables should be chosen and grouped for variety of texture, colour and shape, and between one- and two-thirds of the container should be left bare. Check that the arrangement is interesting and attractive from all sides and remember also to view it from above before leaving.

ABOVE *A substantial piece of ginger forms the foundation of this composition and anchors the two sprays of cotoneaster that arch across and extend it well beyond its wooden base.*

LEFT *Yellow and green peppers gleam voluptuously beneath the dry and papery husk of a corn cob. Three humble Brussels sprouts introduce a further contrast in texture and colour tone, while a single leek rises across them in a dynamic line and falls away elegantly on the farther side.*

ABOVE *The richly patinated surface of this wooden African platter makes a handsome foil for the acid yellow of the lemons which are set at one end against the soft green pile of grapes and decorated with small sprigs of red berries. A single mandarin orange gleams at the other end, with two tiny chrysanthemums.*

SHIKIBANA: LAID FLOWERS

This is something you can do very quickly at the last minute when you have no time to make a proper arrangement. In *shikibana* the flowers and sprays of foliage are laid directly on the table or cloth. The arrangement is made in a moment to last a few hours at most. Since the flowers are not in water it is important to choose material that will survive the evening and will not wilt. A surprising number will last: you can safely use carnations, chrysanthemums, camellias, lilies, orchids, gladioli and freesias.

Lay the foliage first and place the flowers off-centre. Make sure that it looks attractive from all sides and take care to hide the cut ends of branches, flower stems and foliage.

Your guests may be tempted to play with your arrangement. No matter; you can get them to recompose it and share the pleasure you had in making it.

ABOVE *Sprays of bottlebrush run in flowing lines from the single pale pink alstroemeria at the heart of this graceful* shikbana.

RIGHT *This single scarlet carnation against dark, shiny camellia leaves, laid on a crocheted mat, with a spray of pine needles and a cluster of white berries, would add a seasonal note to a Christmas table.*

LEFT *A weightier composition, this arrangement uses berried cotoneaster branches and bright yellow pompon spray chrysanthemums flanked by sprigs of leatherleaf fern.*

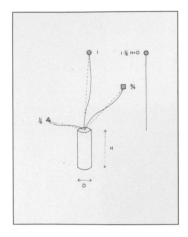

NAGEIRE BASIC UPRIGHT STYLE (LEFT-HAND VERSION)

This left-hand version should go on the left of the surface it stands on, if possible against a plain background so that the lines are clearly seen. It can be placed either low or relatively high but needs some space above because of the strong upward movement of the branches. Do not put it where it is likely to be knocked over by people passing in front of it. Its mirror image, the right-hand version, would of course be placed on the right.

Used in this example: cylindrical stoneware vase with deep brown *tenmoku* glaze and autumn material

Lines 1 and 2 – Cotoneaster 'Cornubia'

Line 3 – small yellow pompon spray chrysanthemum

Filler – variegated privet and conifer

Method of fixing: Lines 1 and 2 – single-bar support; Line 3 – bending

Step 1 The branch chosen for line 1 bent naturally and side branches were removed to leave a single clear line. The stem was placed low down in the vase with the branch resting against the rim and its tip 10° to 15° from the vertical on the left and 10° to 15° forward. The visible part is one-and-a-half times the container size.

Step 2 As neither of the two main divisions of Line 2 gave the right angle, both were left. The lower branch should have been cut shorter. This branch was fixed in the same way as the first in front of the Line 1 branch. The visible part is three-quarters of Line 1 and leans forward left at 45°.

Step 3 The chrysanthemum used for Line 3 was bent to lean forward and rest on the rim at 75° to the left. Because the flowers are such a strong yellow the visible length, seen more clearly in the side view, is only one-third that of Line 2.

Step 4 *After the lines had been checked flowers were added to fill out the arrangement, together with small sprays of variegated privet and conifer. The completed arrangement was then placed in position and topped up with water.*

BELOW *Side view showing the forward movement of the branches and flowers.*

ABOVE *Bird's-eye view showing both the forward and sideward movement of the material.*

CLASSICAL IKEBANA

WHILE CLASSICAL IKEBANA lies outside the scope of this chapter, some classical arrangements have been included, for without some idea of its roots, modern ikebana cannot really be appreciated. If from looking at these arrangements you feel that this is the ikebana you want to learn, you should find a teacher to study with.

There are many schools of classical ikebana. Those represented here are the Ikenobo, the oldest school, and the Koryu, which emerged in the sixteenth century. Like other classical schools,

BELOW LEFT *Classical usubata for formal* seika *on a black-lacquer maki-ashi (curved-leg)* kadai; *bronze tsuri-tsuki, moon vase, on a monkey chain; bamboo vase for informal* seika *on black wooden bases; bronze vase for* chabana *on a bamboo raft; niju-ike, bamboo vase for two-tiered* seika *on a* kadai.

these have developed contemporary styles while continuing to teach the traditional ones.

CONTAINERS

It is not anticipated that you will buy containers like those shown here – even modern replicas are expensive – but the ability to recognize them is helpful. In fact, you should take every opportunity to see Japanese art, either in films or on television, in museums or galleries specializing in Oriental art, at auction sales of Japanese art or, should you be lucky enough to be able to visit Japan, in the country itself. In this way you will develop a feeling for Japanese aesthetics, for its style and use of colour and space, which will greatly benefit your work as you continue to practise.

Classical containers, like the arrangements made in them, are *shin* (formal), *gyo* (semiformal) and *so* (informal).

AN *IKEBONO* ARRANGEMENT

MATERIALS

Modern glass vase with a wide mouth for modern rikka. Wisteria vine, montbretia leaves, pink gladioli 'Meyeii', scabious, sword fern (*Nephrolepsis exaltata*), single-flowered pink *Asparagus densiflorus,* hosta leaves.

BELOW RIGHT *A selection of Japanese baskets for* nageire *and* chabana *arrangements. From left: two modern bamboo baskets: fish-trap basket; basket for summer flowers and grasses; twig basket; latticework basket antique lacquered-bamboo basket; modern basket of black bamboo.*

METHOD OF SUPPORT
KENZAN

This elegant arrangement is a very feminine interpretation of the *rikka* style. The material represents features in a landscape high peak, sunlit slope, shaded valley and so on – but there is no need to understand the symbolism to appreciate the harmony between the lovely arch of the wisteria and the dramatic diagonal sweep of the montbretia leaves, or the graceful positioning of the flowers.

BELOW *More than any other arrangement in the book, this one justifies the claim that ikebana is art.*

CHAPTER 5:
DECORATING WITH PRESSED AND DRIED FLOWERS

*P*RESSED AND DRIED *flowers can be transformed into magnificent designs and arrangements at any time – you can ignore the changing seasons and luxuriate in the delight of working with these challenging and attractive materials. It is especially satisfying to admire the results of your work knowing that you were responsible for every stage of the process. We begin with guidance on the equipment and materials needed to press flowers yourself, including advice on suitable flowers and how to treat them. This section also includes some lovely ideas for your pressed flowers. Then we move on to the fascinating process of drying flowers, telling you everything you need to know, and finishing with a series of stylish dried flower arrangements.*

PRESSING EQUIPMENT AND MATERIALS

ONE OF THE great advantages of this craft is that you can start without spending very much money. In fact, it may well be that you already have most of what you need at home, and that a variety of everyday household objects will now become the essential tools of your craft. It is a good idea to assemble the following items in one place. (Try to keep them there too!)

The most important piece of equipment is, of course, something in which to press the flowers. This could be simply a large book, or it might be a flower press specifically designed for the job.

An out-of-date telephone directory is ideal as a pressing book because it has the right sort of absorbent paper. Books with glossy pages are unsuitable as they can encourage mildew. A second advantage of a phonebook is that it does not matter if its spine is eventually damaged by the thickness of the layers of flowers. (Naturally it would be unwise to use the family bible or any other treasured volume for this purpose!) Whatever large, expendable book is used, additional weight is necessary for successful pressing. Such weight could be provided in the form of other heavy books or bricks.

Although the phonebook method can be perfectly effective, I prefer to use a press. This is because it puts the flowers under greater pressure and therefore speeds the drying process. Also, carefully prepared flowers are rather less likely to be disturbed by having the separate layers of blotting paper and corrugated card placed on them from above, than by the sideways action of closing a book which can easily move the paper.

Many craft shops and quality toy shops now sell flower presses. These are fine – but avoid making the mistake of buying the smallest ones, which measure about 4 in (10 cm) square. The disadvantage of these is that, although they are pretty and can be used effectively for small flowers, they have severe limitations if you want to press such elements as grasses and long, gracefully curving stems. The ideal size for a press is, in my opinion, about 9 in (23 cm) square. Larger ones can become very heavy and, unless they have some special device for maintaining pressure in the middle, the two pieces of wood which sandwich the pressed material may develop a tendency to bow or warp. The result of this is that the flowers in the middle are under less pressure than those around the edge, and are therefore at risk of shrivelling or becoming mildewed.

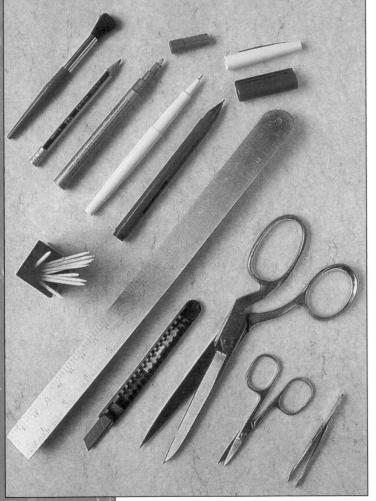

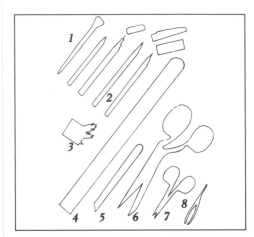

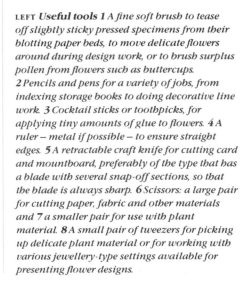

LEFT **Useful tools** 1 *A fine soft brush to tease off slightly sticky pressed specimens from their blotting paper beds, to move delicate flowers around during design work, or to brush surplus pollen from flowers such as buttercups. 2 Pencils and pens for a variety of jobs, from indexing storage books to doing decorative line work. 3 Cocktail sticks or toothpicks, for applying tiny amounts of glue to flowers. 4 A ruler – metal if possible – to ensure straight edges. 5 A retractable craft knife for cutting card and mountboard, preferably of the type that has a blade with several snap-off sections, so that the blade is always sharp. 6 Scissors: a large pair for cutting paper, fabric and other materials and 7 a smaller pair for use with plant material. 8 A small pair of tweezers for picking up delicate plant material or for working with various jewellery-type settings available for presenting flower designs.*

MAKING YOUR OWN PRESS

THIS IS relatively simple and should ensure that you get exactly what you want in size, weight, the number of layers, and so on.

If you are intending to take this craft seriously, you may find it worthwhile to make two or even three presses at the same time, because in the summer months there is often such an abundance of material for pressing that it is hard to manage with only one.

MATERIALS FOR MAKING A PRESS

1   Two pieces of sturdy wood such as plywood, measuring about 9 in (23 cm) square and ½ in (1 cm) thick (9-ply is ideal and should not warp.
2   Four 3 in (8 cm) bolts with wingnuts to fit.
3   Three large sheets of blotting paper.
4   Some stiff corrugated card which can be cut from packing material such as boxes from supermarkets.

Rub down the surfaces and edges of the plywood with sandpaper.

Place the two pieces together, one on top of the other, and drill holes large enough to take your bolts in each of the four corners, about ¾ in (2 cm) from the edge

Fix the bolts into the bottom piece of wood, gluing the heads securely into position.

Cut twelve 8 in (20 cm) squares of blotting paper, trimming off triangular pieces at the corners to accommodate the bolts.

Cut seven pieces of corrugated card of the same size and shape. Starting and ending with card, interleave two pieces of blotting paper with each layer of card.

Place this card and blotting paper 'sandwich' on the wooden base; locate the top piece of wood on the bolts and secure the wingnuts.

You might also find it useful to make a lightweight travelling press, an ideal companion on a country expedition. It can be made on the same principle as the sturdy press, but for convenience it should be smaller – perhaps 6 in (15 cm) × 8 in (20 cm) – and lighter. Substitute thick hardboard for the plywood, and two sturdy tight-fitting elastic bands for the nuts and bolts.

ABOVE *A press in the making.*

ABOVE *A finished press, together with a lightweight travelling press.*

FLOWER COLLECTING

I F YOU ARE lucky enough to have somewhere to grow your own flowers, your work may begin long before the collecting stage. There is the delight of choosing the seed packets most likely to produce blooms good for pressing. Then there are the pleasures of planting the seeds, tending the young plants and watching them grow to maturity.

When collecting flowers for pressing, the aim should always be to pick the best specimens in the best conditions. This is relatively easy with flowers picked very near your home since you can choose just when to pick them. Several factors should be taken into account when deciding on the optimum time for picking.

Flowers must be picked at the right stage in their development. This stage is usually reached shortly after they have emerged from the bud, when their colour is at its richest. Occasionally, buds are more useful to the flower-presser than the open form, as in the case of tightly closed dark-orange montbretia buds. Many designs are enhanced by the use of both buds and open specimens of the same flower, so it is often a good idea to press them in both forms. But do not succumb to the temptation of trying to enjoy the beauty of the flowers on the plant for as long as possible, picking them for pressing only just before they fade or drop. This does give truly disappointing results.

Foliage also has to be picked at the right stage of development. The very young leaves of eccremocarpus, for example, and those of *Clematis montana*

A collection of specimens just removed from the press on their blotting paper sheets.

emerge from the press a striking black colour. If picked when too mature, they turn out a much less inspiring flat green. Even grasses should be watched for the right stage – their delicate spikelets should be open, but not so far developed that they are ready to shed their seeds all over your designs.

Pick each species early in its season when the plants are lush and sappy – you will find that they will press far more successfully than those which appear later in the season.

Another important factor to consider is the weather. Damp is the flower-presser's main enemy: it encourages mildew. Specimens should therefore be collected on a dry day when any droplets of water from the showers of previous days are likely to have evaporated.

The time of day is also important: a sunny afternoon is the best time of all. Even a fine morning may be damp with dew and, by early evening, some flowers will have closed for the night.

The final luxury of picking flowers locally is that it is practical to pick a few specimens at a time and to put them straight into the press before there is any possibility that their condition can deteriorate too much.

When travelling farther afield to collect flowers, it may be more difficult to ensure ideal conditions. However, the guidelines listed above still apply. The major problem is likely to be keeping the flowers fresh. If they have wilted by the time you arrive back home, it will be much more difficult to press them successfully. I can suggest two methods of maintaining freshness.

One is to use a travelling press and press the flowers as soon as possible after picking them, preferably in a sheltered spot. When you arrive home, the card and blotting paper 'sandwiches', with the flowers undisturbed inside, can be

ABOVE *Collecting celandines for pressing.*

simply transferred to the main press. (Alternatively, if the travelling press is not likely to be required again for a while, you can put it under an additional weight and leave it exactly as it is.)

The second method of maintaining freshness is to carry around several air-tight plastic bags. Collect the specimens directly into the bags – not too many in each or they may crush each other. When you have finished collecting, blow air into each bag, as if you were blowing up a balloon, and secure the top with a flexible tie. This air cushion serves to prevent the flowers from becoming crushed, over-heated or dried out. They should then arrive home – even many hours later – as fresh as when they were picked.

Remember to pick only perfect specimens. Pressing cannot improve a substandard bloom – and your designs can only be as beautiful as the individual flowers that make them up.

ABOVE *Collecting forget-me-nots for pressing.*

ABOVE *A collection of flowers sealed in an inflated plastic bag in order to maintain their freshness, as it was not possible to press them immediately.*

LEFT *A perfect buttercup specimen.*

PREPARATION FOR PRESSING

THE FLOWERS and foliage collected will be of many different types, shapes and sizes. It may not always be possible to put them straight into a press without some form of preparation. Various techniques are involved.

The simplest flowers to press are those that are flat or like a shallow dish in shape. Buttercups are a good example of this type and can be persuaded easily into a new two-dimensional state.

Remove any part of a flower which might impair the appearance of the whole after it has been pressed. When flowers are to be pressed in the open form, for example, it is wise to remove stems from all but the sturdiest, in order to prevent them from bruising or deforming the petals under which they lie. For the same reason, certain parts of flowers – like the green calyx which sheaths the back of a primrose are best removed.

Another reason for removing flower parts is to facilitate the transformation into the two-dimensional. Both love-in-a-mist (devil-in-the-bush) and London

Pride press well, once the seedboxes which project in front have been removed. The same can be said of the single dog rose after the careful removal of the seedbox from behind the flower.

Multiple flowers may be prepared in a variety of ways. Some, like elderflowers, can be pressed effectively either as a whole or in small sprays, as long as the groups of florets are spread out as much as possible when being placed in the press. The flower-packed heads of a hydrangea, usually bearing well over 100 florets, may seem a daunting prospect until it is realized that each one can be removed and pressed separately, like any flat flower. One of the multiple flowers which best repays preparatory work is the forget-me-not. If the stems are pressed unprepared, the many flowers – which

had plenty of space in their three-dimensional growing state – will be overcrowded and develop unattractive marks wherever they have overlapped the stem or each other.

If you thin them out, however, you will be doubly rewarded with graceful curving stems of undamaged flowers, and by the individual 'thinnings' which press into tiny circles of sky-blue perfection.

So far, I have considered only flowers that can be converted relatively easily to the two-dimensional. But what of truly three-dimensional flowers like daffodils, roses and carnations? It could be argued that these are best left alone by the flower-presser.

Daffodils can be pressed effectively by removing the seedbox and slicing through the trumpet, after which it is possible to press the two resulting 'profiles'. The same slicing technique can be used on very small rosebuds; larger ones, however, must be treated differently: remove the green sepals for separate pressing, and then carefully peel the

BELOW LEFT *The three-dimensional daffodil can be sliced in two and pressed in profile.*

BELOW RIGHT *All but the smallest rosebuds must be separated into individual petals before pressing. Press the green sepals for the later reconstruction of rosebuds.*

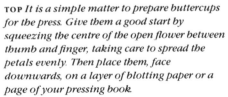

TOP *It is a simple matter to prepare buttercups for the press. Give them a good start by squeezing the centre of the open flower between thumb and finger, taking care to spread the petals evenly. Then place them, face downwards, on a layer of blotting paper or a page of your pressing book.*

ABOVE *It is a good idea to remove both the stem and the calyx of a primrose before pressing. The calyx might otherwise bruise the delicate petal under which it lies.*

TOP *Pressed specimens of flowers that need some preparation before successful pressing can take place.* **1** *Love-in-a-mist and* **2** *London pride should both have their projecting seedboxes removed. The seed box behind the dog rose* **3** *also needs removing. The multi-flowered heads of elderflowers* **4** *must be separated into small sprays while hydrangea florets* **5** *must be pressed individually.*

ABOVE *Forget-me-not stems should be prepared for pressing by removing some of the individual flowers to prevent overcrowding. The spiral of buds at the top of the stem may also be pressed separately.*

delicate satin-smooth petals from the bud so that each one can be pressed individually. (When making rose designs later on, you can reconstruct 'buds' by using petals and sepals, or fully open 'roses' by building up layers of individual petals and using the centres of rock roses as false, but fairly true-to-life, middles – see pages 126.)

Carnations can be treated by the same 'separate petal' procedure. Their pressed petals make realistic green calyx.

It is always sensible to place only flowers of the same thickness in any one layer of the press. This eliminates the risk of putting the flatter ones under insufficient pressure, which could cause shrivelling or encourage mildew. But what if a single flower is itself of uneven thickness? This can sometimes be a problem. One occasionally sees daisies for example whose petals have become spiky because they have not been as heavily pressed as the middles. In the case of such small flowers this problem can usually be overcome by giving the yellow middles an extra firm squeeze before pressing. The solution is not so

ABOVE LEFT *This detail from a wedding bouquet picture shows rose petals reconstructed into open roses and carnation petals in both open flower and bud form.*

TOP *A single daisy-type chrysanthemum being pressed by the 'collar' method.*

ABOVE *Clumps of moss should be allowed to dry out in a warm room for several hours before being separated into small pieces for pressing.*

simple with the bigger daisies, or with other large daisy-type flowers you may want to press. These flowers have middles which are so significantly bulkier than their surrounding petals that it would be impossible to apply even pressure to the whole flower without the use of a 'collar'. This is a series of newspaper or blotting paper circles with the centres cut out to accommodate the thick middle; the correct number of layers of paper should then be placed underneath the petals to even up the thickness so avoiding mis-pressing.

As you gain experience you will develop all sorts of personal techniques for preparing particular flowers and other types of plant material. You may, for example, find it helpful to use a rolling pin to 'pre-press' a particularly thick stem of, say, *Clematis montana*. Alternatively, you may decide to slice it in two before pressing. You will also discover exceptions to the 'rules' — particularly, perhaps, to the one which decrees that all plant material should be placed in the press as quickly as possible. Moss, for instance, almost invariably comes from a damp habitat and is therefore best left in a warm room for a few hours before pressing. It may also be a good idea to allow stems to wilt a little, so that they become more amenable to being pressed as curves.

One final general point about preparation: although you are not necessarily considering the finer details of design at this stage, it is nevertheless helpful to keep the likely eventual design in mind when you are arranging material in the press. Once the specimens are dried, they are more or less fixed in shape. Therefore, any 'persuasion', such as encouraging snowdrop heads to hang at their more natural angle, should therefore be done now.

ABOVE *Position the layers of blotting paper and card in the press taking care not to disturb the flowers being covered.*

PRESSING

THE AIM OF this stage is to dry and flatten the flowers in such a way as to ensure that they come out of the press as bright and as beautiful as when they went in. There are various hazards from which they must now be protected. The three major ones are undue disturbance, mildew and incorrect pressure.

UNDUE DISTURBANCE

Once they have been prepared for pressing, flowers should not be disturbed any more than is absolutely necessary. This means that when the press is being filled, its layers of card and blotting paper must be carefully placed one on top of the other, so that the flowers do not move from the position in which you have set them, and none of the leaves or petals is accidentally folded over. Similar precautions should be taken when closing a pressing book: its pages should be gently rolled closed over the precious contents. You should, particularly in the early days, resist the temptation to 'see how they are getting on'. Partly pressed material is very limp and, once misshapen, is difficult to reshape correctly.

MILDEW

Mildew is the most serious risk at the pressing stage. It can be heartbreaking to open the press after several weeks and find everything inside covered with a damp grey mould. This should not happen if the necessary precautions are taken.

Make sure that flowers are under sufficient pressure. Pressing-books must be adequately weighted, and the wingnuts of presses must be checked every day or two during the first week. This is because as the material in the press dries out, it becomes less bulky so that the nuts need

When using a pressing book, avoid disturbing or damaging specimens by gently rolling closed the pages.

tightening to maintain the pressure.

Keep your presses in a dry, airy place.

To avoid the spread of any mildew if it does occur, make sure that there is plenty of space between the flowers on each layer, and that the layers themselves are well separated by corrugated card or several intervening pages.

Do not add any new, moisture-laden material to a press or book already containing drying flowers.

In spite of my advice not to disturb the flowers unnecessarily, it is nevertheless sensible to inspect a few of them after a week or so to check for damp or mildew. If any is found, a more thorough check is indicated, during which you should throw away any even slightly mildewed specimens, and change damp blotting paper or pressing books.

The pressing process for subjects particularly prone to mildew, such as roses and carnations, may be best *started* in any particularly warm dry place or airing-cupboard. But I would not recommend

this for all flowers, or for any flowers for more than a few days. They can become dry and brittle if left too long.

INCORRECT PRESSURE

Just as too little pressure can put flowers at risk, so over-pressing can also present a problem. It usually occurs only when a press containing layers of corrugated card is used. Such card is normally invaluable because its corrugations aid ventilation and help to prevent the spread of damp. Also its flexible thickness does much to maintain an even pressure on bulky subjects. If precautions are not taken, however, it can cause imperfections on delicate petals. Primroses, for example, pressed between single sheets of blotting paper sandwiched between this card, could emerge from the press with corrugations imprinted on their petals. You may feel happier using the book method for these tender specimens, but you can still use the press if you insert additional layers of blotting paper, or if perhaps you replace the card altogether with several thicknesses of newspaper.

A final note on pressing: it is worth mentioning that both blotting paper and pressing-books can be re-used indefinitely, as long as they are perfectly dry and free from mildew.

WHAT TO PRESS

I**T IS** customary when discussing this craft, to refer to flower-pressing, but of course that term is only a convenient general description of an activity to which there are many aspects. Although flowers will probably be the main elements in most of your designs (and for that reason a survey of flowers takes up a large section of this chapter), the scope of your work will be enormously limited if you have collected only blooms. Foliage of all sorts is needed to give added dimension and interest, and extra possibilities are added by collecting a wide range of other plant material such as stems, tendrils, seeds, seedpods, ferns, grasses, mosses, and even seaweeds.

There are no hard-and-fast rules to predict for certain what will press and what will not, but there are some useful general guidelines. It is helpful to consider these characteristics of each candidate for pressing: its size, shape and degree of succulence.

Unless you intend to make very large pictures, you should be looking for relatively small flowers, avoiding the largest of the cultivated blooms of which gardeners are so justly proud.

Sometimes the beauty of a flower resides largely in its shape, and although it is usually possible to separate the individual petals and reconstruct them in two-dimensional form after pressing, this is not always worthwhile. The beautifully spurred aquilegia (columbine) for example – so descriptively called 'doves round a dish' – is best left alone by flower-pressers who can work more successfully with its flatter-faced relative, the larkspur.

None of the really fleshy flowers – like orchids or the larger lilies – press successfully. Nor do those tender plants

*Snowdrop (*Galanthus nivalis*).*

*Daffodil (*Narcissus minimus*).*

*Alyssum (*Alyssum saxatile*).*

whose high moisture content makes them a prey to the early frosts. (Begonias and the exotic fuchsias fall into this category.) A good test for succulence is to squeeze a flower firmly between finger and thumb. If moisture – or worse still – colour comes out, it is a fair indication that this is a flower to be avoided, for the end result of pressing is likely to be a squashy brown mess on the blotting paper. Conversely, if when squeezing the flower your fingers remain dry, there is reason to proceed with a greater degree of optimism. The sort of flowers that can

be collected most confidently of all are those that can be successfully air-dried. Thus flowers such as larkspur, astrantia and hydrangea, and any of the everlasting varieties that are flat enough, all press and keep colour beautifully.

Once you have a general idea of the sort of flowers to look for, you may proceed with some confidence to experiment with those that are available. The following pages list those that I have found particularly useful. Choosing from these lists may allow you to get off to a good start and help you to avoid some disappointments in the early days, but remember that they are only a starting point. There are many more flowers with pressing potential than those referred to below, and there is no substitute, in terms of interest or reliability, for your own experiments. You will occasionally be disappointed when a small, dry, flattish

*Flowering currant (*Ribes sanguineum*).*

*Forget-me-not (*Myosotis alpestris*).*

*Pansy (*Viola tricolor hortensis*).*

*Poached egg plant (*Limnanthes douglasii*).*

*Rock rose (*Helianthemum nummularium*).*

*Rose (*Rosa *spp.).*

flower, which seemed like an ideal subject for the press, loses all its colour in a short time. But you will, on the other hand, be pleasantly surprised when another less likely subject turns out to be perfect.

The experimentation that I commend to all flower-pressers is very important. If you are unfamiliar with some of the flowers listed below, identify similar members of the same plant family that grow near you and try pressing them instead. Violets and pansies (*Violaceae*), vetches (*Leguminosae*), heathers (*Ericaceae*) and daisies (*Compositae*) are all members of families that have a world-wide distribution. (The composites that I have included in this section should be pressed using the collar method.)

In North America, there are many different species of viola. Perhaps the most immediately attractive is the fern-leaved violet, *Viola vittata,* which is rather like *Viola tricolor.* You might also try some of the large number of North American pea plants (*Leguminosae*) and any heathers that grow in your area. The most obvious composite to try is *Gaillardia pulchella,* otherwise known as Indian blanket, or, more descriptively, firewheels. Both the swamp rose and the prairie rose should press quite satisfactorily and attractively.

Members of all four family groups mentioned above abound in southern Africa. There are many lovely heathers, of which the pink bridal heath, *Erica bauera* and the similarly-shaped green form of *Erica filipendula* seem the most attractive. The selection of available composites is stunning; the many species of arctotis, dimorphotheca and felicia are only a few of the possibilities. You could usefully experiment with any of these with a fair degree of optimism.

In New Zealand and Australia, there is again considerable potential in the vetch and viola families. In the absence of native heathers, try instead the pink *Epacis impressa* and the smaller-flowered white *E. microphylla.* Any everlasting flower flat enough to press is also a candidate for attention, so it would be well worth trying small specimens of the strawflower or yellow paper daisy, *Helichrysum bracteatum* and the soft grey-green flannel flower *Actinotus helianthi.*

The stately buttercups of New Zealand are somewhat fleshier than the European ones, but any flower from this family (*Ranunculaceae*) should at least be the subject of an experiment, as should the smaller varieties of native fuchsia.

Wherever you are, there are flowers that will press. The challenge is to go out and find them. It should not be difficult if you remember the general recommendations given above — that is, if you choose flowers with the right characteristics and are prepared to experiment.

I have arranged the following list of garden flowers roughly in the order of their appearance (in most areas of the world) from early spring to high summer. I think this arrangement may perhaps be a little more helpful than the more usual alphabetical one because, as the seasons progress, you will have an idea of what you might look out for next.

SNOWDROP *(Galanthus nivalis)*
Use only the 'single-skirted' varieties and press in bud or profile. Do not try to press them open because this looks unnatural. Consider using them with the spiky white-lined leaves of the crocus.

FLOWERING CURRANT *(Ribes sanguineum)*
Another spring-flowering shrub, valuable for its small bell-shaped flowers which hang in clusters. Press buds and flowers separately.

SPIREA *(Spiraea arguta)*
A shrub that produces large numbers of tiny white flowers on slender arching stems. Each flower should be snipped off and pressed separately. Later on in the season look out for *S. bumalda,* which produces clusters of crimson flowers.

PRIMULA *(Primula* spp.)
There are many different species of this valuable flower, some of which have a bloom on each stem, whereas others grow in clusters. Most of them are potential 'pressers' and it is well worth while experimenting. The yellow and orange flowers usually press true, while the reds and purples darken. It is advisable to remove the green calyx and to trim off that part of the back of the flower which would otherwise lie behind one of the delicate petals and mark it.

DAFFODIL *(Narcissus minimus)*
In spite of their three-dimensional shape, ordinary daffodils can be pressed by the method described on page 139. It is probably simpler, however, to stick to those varieties of the extensive *Narcissus* family which can be pressed whole. These include the miniature daffodil, named above, which is small enough to be pressed in profile, and the lovely narcissus, 'Soleil d'or', which has several golden flowers on each stem. The trumpet sections of these flowers are relatively flat and will, if you make a few small snips in them, lie against the outer petals so that you can press them open.

FORGET-ME-NOT
(Myosotis alpestris)
Invaluable, and well worth the trouble of snipping off some of the flowers for separate pressing. This creates uncrowded stems which also press well. The spiral of buds at the top of each stem is particularly attractive.

*Delphinium (*Delphinium elatum*).*

*Lady's mantle (*Alchemilla mollis*).*

*Larkspur (*Delphinium consolida*).*

*Love-in-a-mist or Devil-in-the-bush (*Nigella damascena*).*

ALYSSUM *(Alyssum saxatile)*
This is the sweet-smelling yellow alyssum which is often grown together with aubrietia. It is not a marvellous colour-keeper, but is too pretty to pass over completely. Press its minute round buds and tiny, just open, flowers.

PANSY *(Viola tricolor hortensis)*
These are found in many different sizes and colours. (Yellow flowers keep their colour particularly well.) My preference is for the smaller ones and those with the most defined 'faces'.

POACHED EGG PLANT
(Limnanthes douglasii)
A quickly spreading hardy annual, producing dish-shaped flowers which are easy to press and very attractive. Putting one or more directly on top of another intensifies their delicate colour.

ROCK ROSE
(Helianthemum nummularium)
This flowers profusely in the summer sunshine, in a wide variety of bright colours. The petals are fragile but, handled with care, should press perfectly. They are best gathered early in the day for, later on, the petals have a tendency to drop. Do not discard these 'bare' middles however, because they make realistic centres for reconstructed roses.

ROSE *(Rosa* spp.)
I have been surprised to read in more than one book on this craft that pressed roses 'always turn beige or brown'. This need not be so if the petals are pressed individually and are taken from mature buds rather than from open flowers. In the case of miniature roses, it is possible to avoid pressing the petals separately by slicing the buds in two, and pressing each half in profile. The smallest rose of all is the much loved *Rosa farreri perse-*

tosa. This is a single variety, so the tiny buds can actually be pressed whole. They look delightful in simple designs which also use their miniature leaves.

DELPHINIUM
(Delphinium elatum)

This is a tall perennial with colours varying from pale blue to deep mauve. It proudly contradicts the fallacy that blue flowers do not keep their colour. (I have seen pictures of pages taken from a scrapbook over 100 years old in which the delphiniums are still blue!) Each flower on the stem should be pressed individually, but may still be rather large for many designs. If this is the case, wait for smaller flowers on the side-shoots, or consider pressing the petals separately.

LOVE-IN-A-MIST or
DEVIL-IN-THE-BUSH
(Nigella damascena)

Not such a reliable colour-keeper but so beautiful, with its blue flower-head surrounded by fine misty green foliage, that it is still a good choice if mounted on a strong background colour. Remove the seedbox before pressing.

GYPSOPHILA or BABIES' BREATH *(Gypsophila paniculata)*

These sprays of tiny white flowers are very useful as delicate 'space fillers' to soften the outline of designs.

ST JOHN'S WORT
(Hypericum elatum)

This shrub species produces masses of small, yellow, dish-shaped flowers, measuring about 1 in (2.5 cm) across and having a lovely central boss of golden stamens. Remove the seedbox before pressing. The stamens are even more spectacular on the shorter but larger-flowered *H. calycinum,* known as the rose of Sharon or Aaron's beard.

*Gypsophila or Babies' breath (*Gypsophila paniculata*).*

*St John's wort (*Hypericum elatum*).*

*Hydrangea (*Hydrangea *spp.).*

*Peruvian lily (*Alstroemeria aurantiaca*).*

PERUVIAN LILY
(Alstroemeria aurantiaca)

This lovely perennial, which grows in a variety of colours, is a good example of a three-dimensional flower whose individual petals are so beautiful that it really is worth while pressing them separately, prior to reconstructing them into imaginary two-dimensional flowers. I have to admit to having seen them more frequently in florists' shops than in gardens – but perhaps this is something we should try to change, for they are not difficult to grow and the species named above is hardy.

GOLDEN ROD *(Solidago* spp.)

Remove the curved plumes of tiny golden flowers from the tall stems. These may then be used whole, or separated for miniature designs.

HYDRANGEA *(Hydrangea* spp.)

Many species of this plant are excellent for pressing. The pinks, blues, and even the underdeveloped greens press well once the florets have been separated from the densely-flowering heads.

MONTBRETIA
(Crocosmia x crocosmiiflora)

Pick these graceful curving stems when most of the flowers are still in bud. They then retain their deep orange colour. Any of the trumpet-shaped flowers which are already out may be pressed separately, open or in profile.

FUCHSIA *(Fuchsia magellanica)*

The flowers of this bushy shrub are smaller and less moisture-laden than those of most of its exotic relatives. These are the qualities which make it the hardiest of the fuchsias and the best for pressing. Press the lovely pendant flowers in profile, leaving them on their curving stems and taking care to arrange the petals evenly. The scarlet stamens are so striking that you might occasionally choose to use them separated from the flower (for instance as butterfly antennae).

WILD FLOWERS

Before beginning my list of wild flowers, I must emphasize one point. A number of rare species is now protected by law, and in some places it is forbidden to pick even the common ones. The following rules should therefore be observed.

Never pick rare flowers. Never pick even common flowers from places where they are scarce or protected. Remember that if you pick all this year's crop, there will be no seeds for next year. However abundant the flowers may be, never pick more than you need.

DAISY *(Bellis perennis)*

This most indispensable of all wild flowers certainly lives up to its Latin name, for not only does it recur profusely year after year, it also has a long season, in many areas appearing before most flowers we would particularly associate with spring, and continuing to bloom well into the autumn. Moreover, it is an ideal candidate for pressing. The best specimens are those with pink-edged petals.

COLTSFOOT *(Tussilago farfara)*

This is the only one of the dandelion-type flowers to press satisfactorily because, unlike the others, it has a flat middle. It is therefore easy to spread the surrounding spiky 'petals' evenly. Again, it is worth considering using its equally attractive underside.

CELANDINE
(Ranunculus ficaria)

These brilliant yellow starry flowers open their glossy petals to reflect the spring sunshine. They will pale down after a year or so to a lemony-cream colour, but they are so beautiful in form that, if mounted against a dark background, they will still be attractive.

COW PARSLEY
(Anthriscus sylvestris)

This is just one of the many useful species of the Umbellifer family. Others to look out for are fool's parsley, earthnut, burnet saxifrage, rough chervil and wild carrot. All have branched umbels, each topped with 'rays' or clusters of tiny flowers. To make a representation of such intricate structures in paint, embroidery or lace would indeed be work for a patient artist. But nature makes it easy for the flower-presser, by offering us this family of plants, the different members of which adorn the countryside throughout the late spring and summer. Press whole umbels or separate rays.

PRIMROSE *(Primula vulgaris)*

A delicate yellow symbol of springtime. Always remove the green calyx before pressing and use two or more superimposed flowers to intensify the colour of the translucent petals.

HEARTSEASE or
WILD PANSY *(Viola tricolor)*

This small wild pansy has perhaps the most appealing 'face' of any flower. I so much prefer it to its larger cultivated relatives, that I encourage it to grow in my garden. I take care, however, that I plant it in a relatively inhospitable position because plants growing in thin soil produce tiny dark flowers, small enough for the daintiest designs.

SPEARWORT
(Ranunculus flammula)

A very useful small relative of the buttercup, though not as easy to find. Look for it in damp places.

Montbretia (Crocosmia x corcosmiiflora).

Golden rod (Solidago *spp.*).

Fuchsia (Fuchsia magellanica).

Daisy (Bellis perennis).

*Spearwort (*Ranunculus flammula*).*

*Cow parsley (*Anthriscus sylvestris*).*

*Coltsfoot (*Tussilago farfara*).*

*Elderflower (*Sambucus nigra*).*

*Primrose (*Primula vulgaris*).*

*Heartsease or Wild pansy (*Viola tricolor*).*

*Celandine (*Ranunculus ficaria*).*

*Dog rose (*Rosa canina*).*

DOG ROSE *(Rosa canina)*
This charmingly simple wild rose is unlike its lusher, fuller-petalled garden relatives in that it can be pressed whole. Remove the seedbox from behind the flower.

LEAVES
It is possible to make effective designs using leaves only, but though flower pictures without foliage may be pretty, they are bound to look unnatural – for where can flowers ever be seen growing in the absence of greenery?

HERB ROBERT
(Geranium robertianum)
The small purple flowers of this plant are fairly ordinary, but the beautifully-shaped, slightly hairy leaves are invaluable. They are often made even more attractive in the later part of the year by a tinge of red.

EARTHNUT *(Conopodium majus)*
Many members of the Umbellifer family have delicate leaves which press well. This is the most dainty, especially when gathered in the spring, before the white flowers appear. Press as soon as possible after picking, or the leafy sprays tend to wilt and close up.

COMMON MEADOW RUE
(Thalictrum flavum)
The tiny yellow flowers are insignificant but the leaves are beautifully angular. Press both the bright green leaves of midsummer and those which turn yellow as the plant approaches the end of its season.

SILVERWEED
(Potentilla anserina)
This is another indispensable plant, whose feather-edged leaves are grey-green on top and silver underneath.

They can be used whole in large designs and are equally beautiful when segmented into smaller pieces. Silver-leaved plants are generally useful for the attractive variation they bring to designs and because they do not change colour. The following two cultivated plants also offer particularly beautiful silver leaves.

Common ivy or English ivy (Hedera helix).

Ferns.

COMMON IVY or ENGLISH IVY *(Hedera helix)*
Press the smaller leaves of the dark green varieties which keep colour better than the variegated ones.

VIRGINIA CREEPER *(Parthenocissus quinquefolia)*
These beautifully shaped leaves are at their best in their glorious autumn colours.

OAK or ENGLISH OAK *(Quercus pedunculata)*
Press the immature leaves in spring time.

OTHER PLANT MATERIAL
Flowers and leaves are by no means the only suitable subjects for pressing. Other types of plant material are suggested below. The plant names listed under each heading are only a few of the many possibilities.

SEEDS
The loveliest are probably the feathery whirls produced by many of the different varieties of clematis. (I use these not only in flower designs but to form the tails of my cherry-leaf birds.) The winged seeds of the sycamore maple (*Acer pseudoplatanus*) can also be used to make similar simple representations of moths' wings. Some 'natural artists' work only in this medium using attractive seeds, such as those of zinnia, marigold, cosmos daisy, lettuce, grass, reed, caraway and sesame.

SEED-PODS
There are several of these which can be attractively used in two-dimensional designs. Honesty *(Lunaria annua)* produces shiny silver discs when the stems have been dried and the dark outer pods removed. Herb Robert, being a member of the cranesbill family, produces a seed-pod illustrating that name. Even the seedbox of the common poppy *(Papaver rhoeas),* though three-dimensional as a whole, can create a beautiful little 'wooden flower' if its fluted top is carefully sliced off.

FERNS
These grow throughout the world and many of them press satisfactorily. Three that I use regularly are the delicate maidenhair fern *(Adiantum capillus-veneris)* with its lovely sprays of green, and two bigger ferns: the common bracken or brake *(Dryopteris aemula).* Pick young fronds, but consider splitting them into more manageable sizes before pressing. Consider adding variety to designs by the occasional use of the underside of the leaves with their attractive, dark, spore-producing circles.

GRASSES
Most grasses press well because they are fairly dry to start with. For this reason they may conveniently be pressed directly in the books in which they are eventually to be stored.

Some grasses you might consider collecting include: the delicate bents (*Agrostis* spp.) and meadow-grasses (*Poa* spp.) in their many varieties; the aptly named quaking grasses (*Briza* spp.), most useful for flower designs in their smallest form (*B. minor*); the different types of brome (*Bromus* spp.), all of which may be pressed whole and then have their variously shiny or downy spikelets removed for separate use in designs. These spikelets – especially the hairy ones – make realistic 'bodies' for leaf or petal butterflies, as do the individual whiskers of wild oats (*Avena fatua*).

MOSSES
Mosses are especially useful in miniature designs, where small, curving pieces can create the effect that a combination of curved stems and leaves might have made in a larger design. It is not until one begins collecting for the press that one realizes how many different shapes, sizes and shades of moss there are. My favourite ones are the bright green *Eurynchium praelongum,* found commonly on shaded tree-trunks; the darker *Plagiomnium undulatum,* with its intricate tracery of wrought-iron-like shapes, and the sturdier *Mnium hornum.* Because mosses usually grow in very damp places, I prefer to allow them to dry in a warm room for a few hours ·

DESIGN IDEAS FOR PRESSED FLOWERS

ONCE YOU HAVE a collection of good pressed material, you are ready to proceed with confidence to the design stage. Sadly, however, this is just the point at which many people come to a standstill. 'I have books full of pressed flowers, but I've never done anything with them because I just don't know where to begin.' This is a *cri de coeur* heard all too frequently (and I can remember I felt like that too), but now I want to say in reply. 'Don't stop now,

BELOW RIGHT *Make a symmetrical design. Use a selection of regularly shaped flowers and rely on symmetry to produce an attractive effect. The two larger designs are based on anaphalis. The pendant design is made of forget-me-nots and elderflowers.*

BELOW LEFT *Add a little embellishment. Foliage and extra small flowers have been added to the main central flower in each of these three designs. 1 Primrose with golden rod and herb Robert foliage. 2 Larkspur with heather and both silver and green foliage. 3 Limnanthes with cow parsley and fern.*

when you are only a step away from the most rewarding phase of the craft. Have confidence. You will certainly be able to make attractive designs if you let the flowers help you.

The design section of books on flower-pressing, with their references to 'contour', 'balance', 'harmony' and other technicalities can be somewhat daunting to a beginner. I would therefore like to suggest an absolutely practical approach. Of course, this is not the only way to

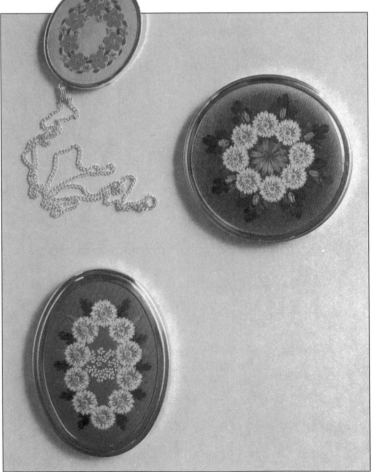

begin, but it will, I hope, build up confidence as you progress. Try working through the following steps, using your own choice of flowers, introducing variations whenever you wish, and abandoning my suggestions altogether at the point at which you find your own style.

START SMALL, START SIMPLE

Choose a small setting and be prepared, at this stage, to rely entirely on the beauty of one individual flower to create the design. Choose your flower with care, for you will not get away with such complete simplicity unless it is a perfect specimen, and unless it is sufficiently intricate or visually interesting to satisfy the eye. Background colour and texture are all-important, and I would recommend the use of fabric for the additional interest it can provide. (Try placing your flower on a variety of different backgrounds to decide which one enhances it most.) Finally, try to ensure that your work is technically perfect, for a badly positioned flower, a roughly cut-out piece of fabric, or a single spot of unwanted glue can mar simple designs.

An ideal flower for this purpose is the astrantia. With its tiny flowers and surrounding pointed bracts, it needs no further embellishment. To add depth to the beautiful pink-tinged specimen used in this paperweight, I have placed it on top of a second, slightly larger, plain green and white flower, and have chosen a pink background to bring out the colour of the central flower.

Another particularly suitable candidate for the simple approach is love-in-a-mist (devil-in-a-bush), with its dark green central stamens and fine misty-green foliage that surrounds the flower. A little judicious rearrangement might be necessary if this foliage is not evenly spread, but basically it is still the simple

beauty of the flower which does the design work.

The lacy flower-heads of the umbellifers are also sufficiently intricate to 'stand alone'. The two species I particularly favour are the wild carrot, used back-to-front to show the beautiful arch-shaped foliage which lies under the flowers, and the burnet saxifrage, with its spoke-like stems. One additional flower-head makes a centre for this design.

You should as you gain experience succeed in making larger and more elaborate pressed flower pictures. But for sheer simple beauty, you may never make anything to surpass these small, one-flower 'designs', in which the patience, care and technique are yours but the art is all nature's.

AND A LITTLE EMBELLISHMENT

Begin again with a single central flower, but this time, use a slightly larger setting and add some pieces of foliage, radiating from the centre. Then introduce some other tiny flowers in colours that blend both with the central specimen and with the background.

In the simplest of the three designs shown, two primroses have been placed one on top of the other to intensify their pale colour. The shape of the petals has been allowed to suggest the position of the five pieces of herb Robert leaf, and three single florets of golden rod, whose deeper colour blends with the pale primroses, have been arranged in each of the spaces thus created.

The Limnanthes design on the darker green also uses two superimposed central flowers, this time with the pale green leaves of a delicate fern in the shape of a six-pointed star, and the heads of cow parsley, making a dainty space-filler.

The design using the central larkspur

is the most complex, using two contrasting types of foliage, with the pink heather florets as space-fillers. (When I first placed this design on its background, I used only four pieces of each type of foliage, but the effect was so square-looking that I added another piece of each.)

ABOVE **Use nature as designer.** *These simple designs show snowdrops and heather just as they grow naturally.*

TABLE MATS

Table mats offer many possibilities for making attractive, personal gifts.

A single beautifully decorated mat is right for some occasions, on others a set would be more appropriate. Sets can be matching or made to individual designs, perhaps with each one linked to a particular month and bearing a suitable inscription.

The backing and the flowers can be chosen to tie in with the colour scheme of the room in which they are to be used or to team with the tablecloth or china. The design on the mats can also be custom-made to suit the recipient's taste, whether modern or traditional or they can be personalized with the initials of the recipients arranged in a daisy-chain fashion, though not necessarily using daisies.

Use thin wood for the backing and stick a protective covering of baize or untreated cork on one side. Paint the top side or cover it with art paper or material then, using tweezers, arrange pressed flowers individually, in prettily placed sprigs or in the chosen design. Fix them in place with a very small amount of transparent adhesive applied on the point of a cocktail stick. When the flowers are correctly positioned press down on them with a clean piece of card to set them in place. Leave the adhesive to set firmly before covering with heatproof heavy glass, Perspex or Plexiglass anchored with strong, clear adhesive or with clips. The edges can be left plain or covered with widths of attractive edging braid.

FLOWER BOOKMARKS

As bookmarks need not be entirely rigid they can be decorated with dried flowers as well as pressed ones. The flowers may be encased in transparent plastic or mounted on a backing of card or coarse linen and then covered with clear plastic film.

To make the edges look attractive, sew around flexible bookmarks and stick bias binding or ribbon around rigid ones. Finish with a length of toning firm ribbon or coloured cord.

GIFT TAGS

Gift tags decorated with dried or pressed flowers add a personal touch to any present but they complete the very special package of a flower-based gift wrapped in flower-scented paper. The gift tag itself can, of course, be made out of paper or card that has been scented with the same flower or used for the decoration. Cut the tag out with pinking shears and add a pretty ribbon of co-ordinated colour.

PRESSED FLOWER PICTURES

Whole blooms, separated petals or a combination of the two can be used to make pictures in whatever style and with whatever theme you choose — simple, natural and countrified sprays, redolent of Victorian drawing-rooms, intricate arrangements with a clever juxtaposition of hues and tints or a modern design that does not appear to have anything to do with flowers.

The backing can be thick art paper, available from art shops, or a material such as hessian or velvet, that will make a good textural contrast to the flowers. Choose a plain colour that will go with the colours of the flowers you intend to use or the room where the picture is to be hung. Avoid anything that is very highly coloured as it will drain the colours from the flowers.

Pressed flowers and petals are very fragile and easily damaged, so to minimize the handling, plan the picture on a piece of paper beforehand and make it up in a place where there are no draughts, central heating or air conditioning ducts, or open windows.

Lightly touch the back of each petal with one of the special adhesives available for handicrafts, and manoeuvre into place with the tip of a small, soft brush. The flowers can be invisibly sealed and protected from the entry of moisture by spraying with an aerosol fixative. The picture can then be covered with glass and placed in the frame.

Pressed flowers can transform many everyday items into attractive, eye-catching, covetable objects. Simply attach carefully placed flowers of a suitable size to any surface that is flat with a very small dab of transparent adhesive applied on the end of a cocktail stick or the point of a fine brush, then protect it with clear adhesive film. This is available from large stationers and art and handicraft shops.

Some of the items that can be decorated with pressed flowers are:

ACCESSORIES
Hair slides and combs

•

Earrings

•

Pendants

•

Brooches

•

Bracelets

•

Ornamental buttons

Matching sets can be made of two or more of these items for a co-ordinated look and the flowers can be chosen so their colours compliment the colours of your clothes.

FOR MEN

Cufflinks

•

Tie pins

FOR THE HOME

*Finger plates – clear glass is
usually used to cover these*

•

Table mats (instructions provided)

•

*Napkin rings – these can match
the table mats*

•

*Gift tags and greeting cards
(instructions provided)*

FLOWER CANDLES

When making the candles, stearin, a combination of animal and vegetable oils, is added to the paraffin wax to prevent the wax dripping when the candles are alight and to aid the distribution of the colourings and the moulding of the candles.

Colourings, candle-maker's essential oils, wicks and moulds are available from craft shops.

ROSE-SCENTED CANDLES

350g/12oz paraffin wax

•

*1 cup dried rose petals, finely crushed
and tied in a muslin bag*

•

35g/1¼oz stearin

•

*⅛ teaspoon pink powdered colouring
or finely grated pink dye disc*

•

*few drops of a candle-maker's
essential oil*

•

wick

•

small flowers or petals, for decoration

Line candle moulds or containers such as straight-sided plastic yogurt or cream cartons or other suitable round or square containers with foil, polythene or cling film. Fix the wicks into the moulds by pushing the wick through a hole in the centre of the bottom of the mould and pulling it through until it reaches the rim. Hold it in place by tying it to a wooden cocktail stick or a fine knitting needle placed across the rim. Seal the hold and secure the other end of the wick with plasticine.

Melt the wax in a bowl placed over a saucepan of hot water but do not allow it to get too hot – it should not exceed 75°C/180°F. Stir in the flowers, then cover. Add the muslin bag of rose petals then, keeping the water in the saucepan warm, leave the flowers to infuse for 40 minutes. Remove the muslin bag.

Melt the stearin in a small bowl placed over a saucepan of warm water. Stir in the colouring and essential oil then stir the mixture into the paraffin wax. Pour most of the wax into the moulds. Leave for about 10 minutes and if wells begin to form around the wick, fill them in with some more wax. Leave to set – this will take about 5 hours.

When the wax has set and is completely cold, remove the mould or the container, breaking or tearing it if necessary. Decorate the sides of the candle with small flowers or petals, fixing them with dabs of warm wax and painting them over with wax to hold them in place and give them a sheen. Keep in a warm, dry place for several days to harden, then polish them with a pad of cotton wool that has been dipped in vegetable oil. Wrap the candles in cellophane or cling film, if liked. The same basic recipe and method can be followed using other flowers. Flowers that have stems can be tied into small bunches and suspended in the wax instead of wrapped in muslin.

375g/13oz of candles, melted down, can be used instead of paraffin wax and stearin.

Your flower candles can have their own holders or candlesticks, specially decorated with pressed flowers – attach them with a very small dab of a clear adhesive then spray with an aerosol film or cover in clear adhesive film.

Bought candles are rather impersonal for a present, but home-made flower candles can show a lot of careful thought. Their scent can reflect the season, such as lilac in spring, or convey a message and the colour chosen to match the rom in which they are to be used. In the bedroom, a candle could be burnt as a sleep and sweet dream inducer on retiring to bed, in the bathroom or lavatory or in the hall as a gently fragrant welcome to a new day.

BELOW *Candles adorned with
pressed flowers. The flowers are affixed
with small amounts of melted wax.*

MAKING YOUR OWN DESIGNS

IF YOU HAVE followed my suggestions so far, you will realize that at every stage, I have offered the diffident artist something to 'lean' on when making designs: the beauty of a single flower; symmetry; nature as a designer; a picture to copy, and so on. But of course, sooner or later, you will want to create something original.

The joy of working with flowers is that you will certainly be able to do this. If you are artist enough to sketch out ideas for designs, either mentally or on paper, so much the better. But if, like me, you are unable to plan in this way, it is still possible to make designs that are both attractive and original. All you have to do is to allow the flowers themselves to make the suggestions. Let me tell you

the story of how my favourite — and most successful — picture came about.

Once upon a time I acquired, from the oddments bin of a local art shop, a sturdy plum-coloured mount. I bought it because it was cheap, and although its colour did not immediately inspire me I was sure that I would eventually find a use for it. I took it home and, several weeks later, decided that the obvious flowers to use with it were the similarly-coloured blooms of my hardy fuchsia. At that point, I really had no idea at all about what sort of design I was going to make. I simply placed the mount over

some white textured paper on to which I then put the fuchsias. I moved them around with the tip of a soft paintbrush, and waited hopefully for ideas. The first thing the flowers told me, quite clearly, was that they had to hang. That is how

BELOW *Learn about balance. Make a picture entirely from leaves. The three slightly curving clematis stems in this picture suggest lines for the eye to follow. All the other leaves — with their lovely variety of shapes, and spring and autumn colours — fan out from these lines. There is, I hope, some sense of movement, as of leaves lifting in the wind, perhaps, and it is reasonably well-balanced. The picture looks different, but still, I think, effective, if you look at it upside down. Further acceptable variations can be achieved by viewing either of the two short sides as possible 'tops'.*

they grow, and any attempt to arrange them otherwise looked unnatural. After a while they began, quite by chance, to assume the character of a weeping tree. I arranged them more definitely into this shape, and gave the tree a 'trunk' made from a straightish clematis stem. I then thought I could enhance the weeping effect by using the fuchsias' own slim leaves in the spaces between flowers.

I was pleased with the effect so far. It seemed to me to be stylized and unreal, a bit like an illustration from an eastern fairy-tale. It was obvious that the design needed a base, and I felt that this should be equally stylized, so I chose to make a 'mound' of tiny, intricately-arranged richly-coloured flowers and foliage. I felt that, to fit in with the style of the whole, the mound should be regular in shape, and I therefore drew a light pencil line around the top of a saucer to make an outline within which to work. I then began to build up pieces of thalictrum foliage and heuchera, heather, lady's mantle and forget-me-not flowers. This was done almost like a jigsaw puzzle, fitting in each piece as closely as possible to the next but without the pieces touching or overlapping each other.

I have to admit that when I had finished making this picture, I was delighted with it. The style, I knew, would not be to everybody's taste, but I liked it, and I had the pleasure of knowing that it was my original design. Of course the truth is that when I began the picture I had no idea how it would turn out. I am therefore grateful to the flowers for showing me what to do, and for liberating the frustrated artist in me.

There is a happy postscript to this story. A year or so after I had begun making 'fuchsia trees', a customer who had bought one of the earliest versions, decided that she would like another picture to make up a pair: the same size, the same colours, the same style, but a different picture. Initially, I was a bit frightened by this request. I knew I should be aiming at a second stylized tree, but at that stage had no further idea what it should look like. I therefore decided to see if the flowers could, once again, come up with some ideas. This time I chose pink larkspur, as having flowers of the right colour, on which to base the matching picture. And again, as I moved them around, the idea came – this time at the point where they formed themselves into a rough circle which looked vaguely like a standard rose-tree. I picked up this suggestion, and introduced miniature rose leaves as 'rosebuds'. The fuchsia tree had a partner. And they lived happily ever after!

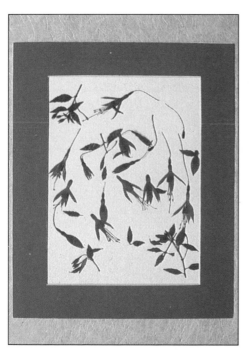

Fuchsia tree. 1 *Flowers and foliage are placed on a white background.*

2 The flowers begin to suggest that they should hang.

3 The trunk and some leaves are added.

The point of this story is to prove that there is no need to start with a clear idea of the sort of design you want to make. You can simply take some carefully pressed flowers and foliage, and place them on a background colour that enhances their beauty, inside a frame or mount that suits both flowers and background. Then all you have to do is move them around until they suggest ideas. You will not have to wait for long – for I am quite certain that I am not unique in getting some of my best design ideas directly from flowers. Give it a try!

Finally, as a footnote to this section, I should say one more thing. You may be puzzled by the fact that I appear to be flouting my own 'rules' by sticking flowers on a white background and using a mount that keeps them away from the glass. There are, of course, always exceptions to rules, and I have chosen to go on using white paper in this case because its starkness seems to be right for the 'fairy-tale' effect of these pictures, and because experience tells me that small, hardy fuchsias and larkspur are excellent colourkeepers which do not fade and disappear into their background. Also, both these flowers are so sturdy that as long as they are well stuck down, they should not suffer from the lack of direct pressure.

ABOVE *The completed picture illustrated on the previous page as a step-by-step.*

FAR LEFT *A partner for the fuchsia tree (made from pink larkspur and miniature rose leaves).*

LEFT *A seed picture, in which the tawny owl is fashioned mainly from hogweed seeds, with pear pips (seeds) for eyes, the curved seeds of marigold for 'eyebrows' and cosmos daisies for claws.*

PURCHASED SETTINGS

IMAGINATIVE CRAFT suppliers are offering an ever-widening variety of settings in which work can be mounted. These range from small, relatively inexpensive items, like pendants and pill boxes, to some special products such as individually-turned wooden bowls and hand-cut lead crystal jars, for favourite designs or special gifts.

These purchased items have four great advantages: they are usually round or oval – the ideal shapes for flower work; they can generally be assembled quickly and easily, leaving more time to concentrate on designs; they are, for the most part, well made so that good flower work mounted in them has a really professional appearance; and finally, when presented as gifts, they are more than just flower designs: they are attractive in themselves and, in many cases, useful.

The components and assembly procedures for the settings described on the subsequent two pages are common to most of them, and can usefully be dealt with in a general introduction.

First prepare the design background. This is simple if the work is to be mounted directly on to the manufacturer's design card. I prefer to use a fabric background because of the range of colours and textures available. I therefore use the design card simply as a template around which to cut my material (usually velvet or satin). Before cutting out, it is advisable to back the fabric with a self-adhesive covering material (clear or patterned – it will not show). This gives it more body and makes it generally easier to handle.

Then make the design. This should suit the shape of the frame and the purpose for which it is intended. (The lid of a

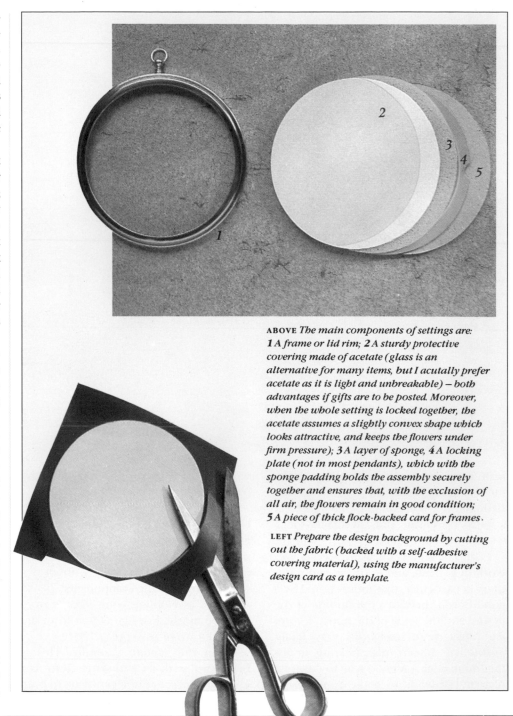

ABOVE *The main components of settings are:*
1 A frame or lid rim; 2 A sturdy protective covering made of acetate (glass is an alternative for many items, but I acutally prefer acetate as it is light and unbreakable) – both advantages if gifts are to be posted. Moreover, when the whole setting is locked together, the acetate assumes a slightly convex shape which looks attractive, and keeps the flowers under firm pressure); 3 A layer of sponge, 4 A locking plate (not in most pendants), which with the sponge padding holds the assembly securely together and ensures that, with the exclusion of all air, the flowers remain in good condition; 5 A piece of thick flock-backed card for frames.

LEFT *Prepare the design background by cutting out the fabric (backed with a self-adhesive covering material), using the manufacturer's design card as a template.*

mahogany box made for a man's study, for example, should have an altogether stronger, less delicate design than that of a pink porcelain pot, designed for a woman's dressing table.)

I think it important in pressed-flower work in general, and in these dainty settings in particular, that there should be a good border between the outline of the design and the edge of the frame. (Nothing looks more haphazard than badly positioned flowers disappearing under the frame edge.) A good way to ensure a regular border is to make your design with the frame actually fitted around the background while you are working.

It is necessary to stick down each item because although the assembly will eventually hold the flowers firmly in place, it is almost impossible to transfer unfixed work into a setting without disturbing some of the components.

Before assembling your work, ensure that the finished design is free from unwanted 'bits' of any sort.

Clean the acetate carefully. This is best done with an anti-static cloth. For good measure, breathe gently on to both

ABOVE *Ensure a regular border around your work by making the design with the background actually fitted inside the frame.*

ABOVE RIGHT *Use firm thumb pressure to ensure that the locking plate is pushed firmly home. This is an important process in the assembly of these settings.*

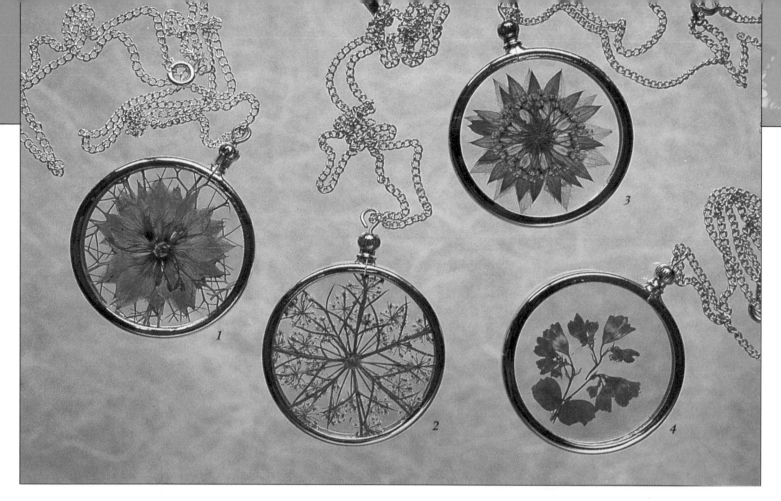

ABOVE *Transparent pendants (1½ in (3.8 cm) in diameter). The flowers are: 1 love-in-a-mist, 2 wild carrot, 3 astrantia, 4 heuchera.*

BELOW *Pill-box and ashtray designs ranging from the simplest single flower like the astrantia 1; through designs which add embellishment to one main flower 2 daisy, and 3 heartsease; to the delicate crescent arrangement of forget-me-nots and London Pride 4; and the intricate design of lobelia, heuchera and alchemilla.* **5.**

acetate and design immediately before assembly.

Place the acetate in the frame, and the design, face downwards, against it.

Place the sponge padding in position, and then insert the locking plate, raised side towards the design. Firm thumb pressure is needed all round the perimeter to push this firmly home.

Insert the thick flock-backed card into the frame, or lid liner into the lid. The liner should be held in position with adhesive or some double-sided sticky tape.

ABOVE *Four simple heather designs illustrating the size and shape of four of the most useful gilding metal frames available. These ovals measure a) and b) respectively 4½ in (11.5 cm) × 3½ in (8.9 cm) and 3¾ in (9.5 cm) × 2½ in (6.1 cm). The round frames c) and d) respectively are 3 in (7 cm) and 4 in (10.2 cm) in diameter.*

ABOVE RIGHT *Three harmonizing larkspur pictures in a range of pinks and blues.*

Handbag mirrors. These offer an even greater scope for design than the small circular pictures they resemble. Whereas the phlox and heuchera design (centre) would look equally good as a hanging picture, the symmetrical anaphalis design (right) might be too formal for such a setting. This regular design is, however, ideal for a mirror setting.

ABOVE LEFT *A 4 in (10 cm) gilt box containing a sewing kit. The simple lid design shows love-in-a-mist on a blue velvet background.*

TOP RIGHT *Pink and blue designs look particularly good in silver-plated settings such as these 3 in (7.5 cm) trinket boxes. These designs are made with daisies and forget-me-nots on pink velvet, rock roses and heuchera on pale satin and burnet saxifrage on royal blue velvet.*

ABOVE RIGHT *A matching silver-plated trinket box and oval frame each showing a highly intricate design of lobelia, heuchera and alchemilla.*

SETTING FLOWERS IN RESIN

APPLYING THE COLOURED BASE LAYER

MEASURE EXACTLY equal parts of the two resins into the mixing vessel. This is best done by pouring a small quantity from each bottle into separate containers, and then using separate hypodermic syringes to draw off exact amounts. Only very small quantities are required, totalling no more than 2 tsp (10 ml), because the components are all small and the mix remains workable only for about 20 minutes.

Stir thoroughly for two to three minutes, making sure that the stirring stick comes into contact with the whole surface area of the container as well as with the fluid in its centre. Take care to lift the fluid from the bottom so that this too is blended.

Add colour paste in very small amounts until the background colour you want is attained. You can, of course, mix colours for a variety of effects. Lovely pale shades can be made by adding tiny amounts of red, green or royal blue to a basic white mix.

Ensure that the components are dust-free and lying completely flat.

Use a cocktail stick to apply a thin layer of resin in the required colour to the base of each item.

Allow this coat to cure for at least 24 hours in a curing cabinet or warm room before going on to the next stage.

MAKING THE FLOWER DESIGNS

This is carried out in just the same way as for other miniature designs. Apply tiny amounts of glue to the back of the thickest part of each flower or leaf, and stick it to its coloured resin background. (Any unsecured item will float when the covering layer of resin is applied!)

APPLYING THE CLEAR COVERING LAYER

Keep the designs in their levelling devices and repeat the measuring and stirring steps as above, this time keeping the resin clear.

Use a cocktail stick, first to apply drops of resin to the design and then to

*Applying the coloured base layer **1** Draw off exact amounts of each type of resin using a different hypodermic syringe for each.*

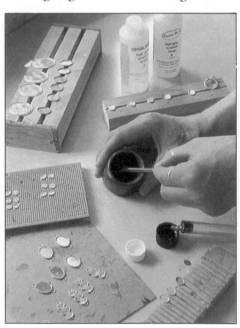

2 Stir thoroughly.

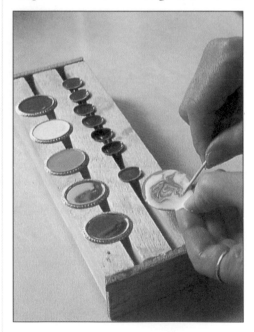

3 Add the colour paste in very small amounts. A tiny quantity of the royal blue paste is here being added to basic white mix to achieve an attractive pale blue.

4 Use a cocktail stick to apply a thin layer of coloured resin to the base of each item.

The flower design is made in just the same way as when other backgrounds are used. Each item is stuck down with a tiny amount of glue.

Apply the clear covering layer of resin with a cocktail stick.

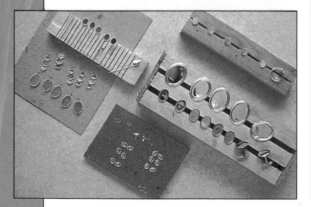

make sure that the whole area is covered. Aim for a slightly convex finish. (The surface tension of the resin prevents the higher central part from flowing over the edges.) Even when the middle of a flower has been firmly glued down, it is possible that the outer edges of delicate petals may float upwards in the resin coating. This creates a very attractive three-dimensional effect and is no problem as long as the petal edges do not break through the surface of the resin.

LEFT CENTRE *As components increase in size (these pendants are ³/₄ in (1.8 cm) high, it is possible to introduce slightly larger flowers. Used here is a spray of heuchera, heartsease, anaphalis and cow parsley.*

LEFT *When making designs for cuff-links, you may well be trying to achieve a plainer, more masculine effect. Try using grasses or heather against strong dark backgrounds.*

It is important that this clear coating has a smooth finish and is bubble-free. If bubbles appear, help them to rise to the surface and burst by gently blowing or breathing on them. You might even apply a little heat from a hair-drier held some 10 in (25 cm) away from your work. Stubborn bubbles may respond only to being pierced with a pin.

Return designs to the curing cupboard for at least 24 hours. The resin cures fully in about a week.

METHODS OF DRYING FLOWERS

IF YOU HAVE ever walked around a beautiful and well-stocked garden in summer and wished you could capture the ambience for ever – you can. Drying flowers and preserving foliage are ways of suspending nature, of holding plant materials at the peak of their condition and in all their glorious array of colour.

Until you have time to build up a selection of materials you have preserved for yourself, specialist shops offer an ever-increasing array of dried flowers and seedheads, a tapestry of different textures, shapes and sizes that enable you to start designing with flowers straight away.

But no shop-bought materials can give you quite the same satisfaction as those you have chosen to preserve for yourself, and no shop can offer the range that you can gradually build up by cutting a few stems from a garden here and a hedgerow there. Add those to the exotic materials you can buy, and the repertoire of materials at your fingertips will be enormous.

HANGING FLOWERS TO DRY

The techniques for preserving flowers, seedheads, and leaves are encouragingly simple: the principle method involves nothing more than hanging the materials in a warm, airy room. Store them in a dry place, position arrangements away from the full glare of sunlight, and the flowers should retain their charm and colour for years to come.

If you are gathering materials for drying or preserving, the stage of their development at which you harvest them, and even the time of day, is crucial. You need to capture most flowers just before

Flowers and seedheads make an attractive decoration in a room corner as they hang in bunches to dry.

they are fully opened. In the case of larkspur, for example – one of the prettiest of tall-stemmed flowers for dried arrangements – this means cutting them when some of the topmost florets are still in tight bud, and only the lowest ones are fully open. Everlasting flowers such as helichrysum and helipterum should be cut as soon as they start to dry on the plant, when they feel crisp and papery. Roses are a special case: snip them when the buds are only just beginning to unfurl.

It is important to cut all materials for preserving on a dry day, after the morning dew has dried and before the evening dew has settled. Midmorning and late afternoon are the best times. Plant material cut at high noon, when the sun is at its strongest, tends to wilt and lose its natural form.

Air drying is by far the most widely practised method of preserving, and one that is suitable for the widest range of materials. According to type, you hang the material in small bunches, place stems flat on a shelf or rack, or arrange them loosely to stand upright in a container. Whatever the method, put them in a dry, warm place that has a free circulation of air. An airing cupboard, the space over the boiler, or a dark corner in a well-heated room are all suitable locations.

To prepare the materials for drying, strip off the lower leaves, which would create unnecessary condensation in the drying room, and sort the material according to type.

Flowers suitable for hang-drying, either singly or in small bunches, include all the everlastings, such as statice, sea lavender, and helichrysum; those composed of a mass of small florets, such as larkspur, marjoram, lady's mantle *(Alchemilla mollis)*, yarrow, mimosa, and golden rod; those composed of a mass of petals, such as cornflower, peony, zinnia, and rose; and a wide range of seedheads, including love-in-a-mist, poppy, lupin, mallow, and Chinese lantern.

Tie the bunches with a slip knot in raffia or fine twine, and hang them on a pole, a rack, on books or wire coathangers, whichever is most convenient. Check the bunches every couple of days and tighten the knots as the stems dry and shrink. The materials will take several days to dry; the exact timing will, of course, depend on their substance and moisture content and on the temperature and humidity of the drying area which you are using.

Some plants with a heavy head-to-

A basket of dried rosebuds.

stem ratio dry more successfully if they are placed flat on a rack (a slatted shelf in an airing cupboard is ideal), or on absorbent paper on a shelf or in a box. This category includes all grasses, dock, giant hogweed, and lavender, which is less inclined to shed its seeds this way than when dried by hanging.

A third category of plants dries most successfully by standing upright in a wide-necked container — wide-necked so the stems can fan out, allowing the warm, dry air to circulate freely around all the heads. Acanthus, gypsophila, bulrush, and hydrangea are among those plants best dried in this manner.

An alternative way to dry multi-petalled flowers such as cornflower, zinnia, and pearl everlasting and hydrangea, is by air and water drying. For this method, stand the stems in a container with a little water, and leave them undisturbed until it has evaporated. Then remove the stems, wipe them dry, and place them in an airing cupboard for a day or two in order to discourage mould.

A few plant types form a separate section within the upright drying category. These include sweetcorn, globe artichoke, carline thistle, protea, and garlic and onion seedheads, which need support just beneath the head. You can use the slats in an airing cupboard, or a piece of chicken wire stretched across a frame. Push the stalks through the holes so the heads rest on the surface, and leave them to dry for several days.

USING DESICCANTS

Some flowers are more successfully dried in desiccants, or drying agents. These include all flowers with an open, saucer-like shape, such as buttercup; trumpet and cone shapes; and multi-petalled composites of the daisy type (gerbera and marguerite, for example). For the drying agent you can use ground silica gel (you can buy it in the form of blue crystals, and crush it with a rolling pin or in a pestle amd mortar), household borax, sifted to remove any lumps, alum powder, and dry silver sand. While ground silica gel and, for the largest of flowers, silver sand can be used alone, both borax and alum are most effective when mixed in the proportion of three parts of the chemical to two parts sand.

The desiccant method of drying greatly extends the range of flowers you can preserve, and includes pansy, daffodil, narcissus, freesia, lily, ranunculus, anemone, camellia, and orchid. Some other flowers that may be air-dried give better results when preserved in this way, roses and peonies are examples.

To prepare flowers for desiccant drying, cut woody stems to within about 1 in (2.5 cm) of the calyx, and cut off fleshy stems at the flower base. It is easier to mount the now stemless flowers on short lengths of wire at this stage, while they are still supple, than to leave it until they are dry and brittle. Push a short length of medium-gauge stub wire through the base and in to the flower or floret centre. Once they are dry, you can mount the short woody or wire stems on longer wires or thin split canes.

The method of desiccant drying is simple. Pour a ½ in/1.5 cm layer of the dry crystals or powder in to the base of

Flashes of bright yellow helichrysum and bunches of achillea complete this simple yet effective design.

1 To wire flowers before drying, remove most of the stem and push stub wire through the flower centre. Coil the extra wire around the base of the flower for support.

2 Cover the bottom of a deep, airtight container with the dessicant. Lay the flowers on it according to their shape and size – smaller flowers face down, and larger ones on their sides.

3 Gently sift or pour the dessicant over the flowers, allowing it to fall between the petals and on to the flower centre. Continue until the flowers are completely covered.

4 Close the container with an airtight lid and leave in a warm, dry place. When the crystals turn from blue to white, the flower moisture has been absorbed.

5 Carefully pour off the dessicant. If the flowers are ready, they will feel papery and completely dry. If not, replace them in the crystals for a little longer.

6 When drying intricate or delicate flowers, it may be necessary to brush away any remaining dessicant between the petals with the point of a fine paint brush.

an airtight tin or box, and place the flowerheads, arranged so they do not touch, on top. Then allow the desiccant to trickle slowly through your fingers or a paper cone on to the flowers, so that it comes into contact with every part of each petal. Use a spoon or brush to complete the cover-up job, then slowly

trickle a thin layer of desiccant over the top. Cover the box and leave it undisturbed for at least two days; for large flowers such as double dahlias and chrysanthemums it's best to leave them for up to 10 days.

To test for readiness, use a small camel-hair brush to ease the desiccant away

from the flowers. When dry, they should feel as crisp as tissue paper. Carefully remove the flowers from the container; at this stage, when all the moisture has been drawn from the petals, they are extremely brittle and can be easily damaged. Use the brush again to gently remove any desiccant particles.

PRESERVING IN GLYCERINE

Preserving foliage and bracts in a glycerine solution enables you to add a whole range of glossy materials to your dried collection. With their enhanced autumnal colours and glowing surfaces, such materials blend well with both fresh and dried flowers.

Use the technique on sprays and deciduous leaves such as copper beech, beech and oak; on evergreen leaves such as senecio, privet, ivy, laurel, eucalyptus, mahonia, magnolia, holly, and blackberry; and on heathers and the flower-like bracts of hydrangea and bells of Ireland, *Molucella laevis.*

Deciduous leaves to be preserved in glycerine should be cut in early summer, when the sap is still rising in the plant. Evergreen leaves can be harvested at almost any time of year, but avoid early spring, when the new young shoots are pale green and vulnerable.

Prepare plant material by removing the lower leaves and any damaged ones. Cut the base of the stems at a sharp angle to expose the maximum surface area to the preserving solution. Split or lightly hammer the ends of hardwood stems, and scrape any about 2 in (5 cm) of the bark so they can more readily take up the fluid. Stand the stems in water for about two hours to condition them and give them a long drink.

Make a solution of four parts glycerine to six parts very hot water. Mix it well, and pour it in to deep containers to a depth of about 3 in (7.5 cm). Stand the stems in the solution, pushing them well down so the ends are completely immersed, and transfer the containers to a cool, dark place for several days. As the stems take up the solution, the water will evaporate and the glycerine will become absorbed by the leaves or bracts,

leaving them supple and shiny. Check the material after about six days. It is ready once droplets of glycerine appear on the surface.

Wipe the leaves or bracts and stems dry with a clean cloth. Sieve the glycerine solution, and pour it in to an airtight jar for later use.

Large individual leaves such as laurel, magnolia, fig and *Fatsia japonica* may be preserved by total immersion in a half-and-half glycerine and hot water solution. When the leaves have darkened in colour and feel very pliable, remove them and wash in soapy water. Dry thoroughly, and store them between tissues. To mount the leaves on false wire stems, thread a stub wire in and out along the central vein.

The preserving process considerably darkens leaves and bracts, turning some chestnut brown, some deep beige, and others nearly black. You can bleach them by leaving the material on a sunny window-sill for several weeks, after which most leaves and bracts will have faded to a warm cream or deep parchment colour.

If colour is important to your collection, and especially if you long to capture all the vibrant shades of fallen leaves, you can do so by pressing them. Leaves dried by pressing will become brittle but, once they are threaded on wires, they can be used to spectacular effect in dried flower arrangements. What pressed leaves lack in suppleness, they make up for in their exciting variety of colour, from the fiery red of Virginia creeper to the soft gold of field maple, from the greeny yellow of chestnut to the bronzy yellow of the tulip tree, or whitewood.

ABOVE *A small willow basket filled with dry foam holds a nosegay of dried flowers and seedheads, including majoram, yarrow, tansy and love-in-a-mist.*

OPPOSITE *A small posy of dried rosebuds, sea lavender and lime-green* Alchemilla mollis *decorates the back of a bedroom chair.*

PLANT MATERIALS TO DRY

THE FOLLOWING TABLE is a guide to some of the plant materials you can dry by the methods described. It is, of course, by no means a complete list of all the possibilities, which are endless.

MATERIAL	PART OF PLANT MATERIAL TO BE DRIED	METHOD
Acanthus	flower	air drying
Achillea	flower	air drying
Anemone	flower	desiccant
Astilbe	flower	air drying
Bell heather	flower	air drying
Bells of Ireland	bracts	air drying and glycerine
Broom	short flower sprays	desiccant
Bulrush	seedhead	air drying
Buttercup	flower	desiccant
Camellia	flower	desiccant
Campion	flower	air drying
Carnation	flower	desiccant
Celosia cockscomb	flower	air drying
Chamomile	flower	air drying
Chinese lantern	seedhead	air drying
Chive	flower	air drying
Chrysanthemum	flower	desiccant
Clematis	leaves and seedheads	air drying
Copper beech	leaves	air drying and glycerine
Cornflower	flower	air drying and microwave
Daffodil	flower	desiccant
Dahlia	flower	desiccant
Daisy	flower	desiccant
Delphinium	flower	air drying and desiccant
Dock	seedhead	air drying
Dryandra	flower	air drying

MATERIAL	PART OF PLANT MATERIAL TO BE DRIED	METHOD
Eryngium	flower	air drying
Fennel	leaves	microwave
Fescue grass	seedhead	air drying
Feverfew	flower	air drying and microwave
Forsythia	short flower sprays	desiccant
Giant hogweed	seedhead	air drying
Globe artichoke	seedhead	air drying
Glove amaranth	flower	air drying
Golden rod	flower	air drying
Grape hyacinth	flower	desiccant
	seedhead	air drying
Gypsophila	flower	air drying
Holly	leaves	skeletonising
Honesty	seedhead	air drying
Hop	leaves and flowers	air drying
Hydrangea	bracts	air drying
Ivy	leaves	skeletonising
Jerusalem sage	flower, leaves and seedhead	air drying
Laburnum	short flower sprays	desiccant
Lady's mantle	flower	air drying
Larkspur	flower	air drying and desiccant
Laurel	leaves	skeletonising
Lavender	flower	air drying
Lilac	small flower sprays	desiccant
Lily	flower	desiccant
Lily of the valley	flower	desiccant
London pride	flower	desiccant
Love-in-a-mist	flower and seedhead	air drying
Love lies bleeding	seedhead	air drying
Lupin	seedhead	air drying

MATERIAL	PART OF PLANT MATERIAL TO BE DRIED	METHOD
Magnolia	flower	desiccant
	leaves	skeletonising
Mallow	seedhead	air drying
Marjoram	flower	air drying and microwave
Millet	seedhead	air drying
Mimosa	flower	air drying
Narcissus	flower	desiccant
Old man's beard	leaves and seedhead	air drying
Onion	seedhead	air drying
Pampas grass	seedhead	air drying
Pansy	flower	microwave
Peony	flower	air drying or desiccant
Pine	cone	air drying
Pink	flower	air drying
Polyanthus	flower	desiccant
Poppy	seedhead	air drying
Pot marigold	flower	air drying and desiccant
Quaking grass	seedhead	air drying
Ranunculus	flower	desiccant
Rose	bud, flower and leaves	air drying
	fully-opened flower	desiccant
Rue	seedhead	air drying
Sage	flower	air drying
	leaves	air drying and microwave
Sea lavender	flower	air drying
Sedge	seedhead	air drying
Senecio	leaves	air drying and microwave
Silver-leaved everlasting	flower	air drying
Sorrel	seedhead	air drying
Statice	flower	air drying

MATERIAL	PART OF PLANT MATERIAL TO BE DRIED	METHOD
Stock	flower	desiccant
Strawflower	flower	air drying
Sweetcorn	seedhead	air drying
Sweet pea	flower	desiccant
Sunray everlasting	flower	air drying
Tansy	flower	air drying
Timothy grass	seedhead	air drying
Wallflower	flower	desiccant
Winged everlasting	flower	air drying
Zinia	flower	desiccant

The sepia colour of this arrangement reflects the portraits beneath it.

The montbretia stems, moss and achillea head are enhanced by this unusual handmade container.

POT POURRI

MAKING POT POURRI is an extension of the art of drying flowers, and adds another dimension to decorating the home. A bowl of tactile, colourful pot pourri is a delightful and natural way to scent a room. Rustle the flowers and petals with your fingers and you release the fragrance, a waft of an aroma that, according to the ingredients, can remind you of a herb garden on a summer's evening or conjure up images of the mystical Orient.

Traditionally, pot pourri is made of scented flowers such as roses, lavender, pinks, sweet pea, jasmine, honeysuckle, hyacinth, freesia and orange blossom, and aromatic leaves such as bay, rosemary, lemon thyme, lemon balm, rose geranium, marjoram and peppermint. You can also add a few favourite flowers for their shape and colour – larkspur, perhaps, for its intense blueness and marigold petals for their brightness.

Your kitchen spice rack will yield many of the popular spices that give pot pourri the depth of its aroma. These include cardamom, coriander, cinnamon, allspice, mace, nutmeg, cloves and star anise.

To hold the scents of the dried plant materials and spices you need a fixative such as dried orris root powder which is available from herbalists and some chemists, and to intensify the aroma you need a few drops of an essential plant oil, such as rose, lemon or neroli.

Smaller amounts of other scented ingredients are added to give depth to the perfume. Such ingredients include scented leaves like the sweet geraniums, bay, lemon balm and marjoram, spices and dried fruit peels.

Cinammon, cloves, allspice, nutmeg, mace, coriander and cardamom are the most frequently used spices. Whole spices should be freshly coarsely ground or crushed in a pestle and mortar as ready-ground spices soon lose their aroma and will stick to the sides of glass containers. Occasionally, whole cloves, whole coriander seeds, pieces of mace and small pieces of cinnamon stick are added for appearance's sake.

Essential oils, available from chemists and herbalists must be added drop by drop and the ingredients stirred after the addition of each drop as they are very powerful and will spoil the balance of the perfumes if added in too-large amounts. It is better to use a combination of oils than a larger amount of one type if making large amounts of pot-pourri.

An ingredient that will prevent the pot-pourri mixture from decaying is also necessary. Bay salt used to be used but nowadays a non-iodised salt, such as sea salt, is normally incorporated. Dry it in a low oven for several hours before using it.

A small cotton or muslin sachet of silica gel buried in a pot-pourri mixture will help to keep it dry.

ROSE POT-POURRI
DRY
450g/1lb freshly picked scented rose petals
100g/4oz rose geranium leaves
100g/4oz freshly picked jasmine
100g/4oz freshly picked lavender flowers
1 teaspoon lemon thyme
1 teaspoon orris root powder
1 teaspoon ground cloves
1 teaspoon dried lemon peel
1/2 teaspoon dried orange peel

5 drops rose oil
2 drops jasmine oil

Dry the fresh flowers. Using your hands mix the flowers, lemon thyme, orris root, spices and fruit rinds together in a glazed earthenware pot gently but thoroughly. Add the oils drop by drop, mixing well after each addition. Keep tightly covered for about 6 weeks, gently stirring the ingredients occasionally. Distribute the mixture between containers.

SWEET-SCENTED POT-POURRI
DRY
100g/1oz dried scented rose petals
25g/1oz dried lily of the valley
25g/1oz dried clove pinks
25g/1oz dried sweet peas
15g/1/2oz dried rosemary
15g/1/2oz dried thyme
2 tablespoons crushed dried lemon rind
2 tablespoons crushed dried orange rind
1 tablespoon bruised cloves
4 tablespoons powdered orris root
5 drops of bergamot

Mix the first nine ingredients together and leave for 2 days. Stir in the gum benzoin and orris root then the oil of bergamot, drop by drop. Cover tightly and leave for 6 weeks, stirring occasionally. Transfer to china or glass bowls.

STEP-BY-STEP DRIED FLOWER ARRANGEMENTS

EVERLASTING PLEASURE

MATERIALS

Basket, plastic prong, florist's clay, dry foam, raffia ribbon, stub wire (to attach ribbon). Wheat, dried larkspur, dried rosebuds.

1 A plastic spike fixed to the base of the basket with a dab of florist's clay holds in place a piece cut from a block of dry foam. A fan shape of wheat ears begins the posy design.

2 Colour is added with short-cut stems of pink larkspur, one of the prettiest of dried flowers. Wheat stalks are inserted at the other end to give the illusion of a posy.

3 A handful of pink rosebuds completes the charming posy design, an arrangement that would make a delightful birthday or anniversary gift. The bow is made from a strip of raffia paper ribbon, cut to one-third of the original width.

3

1

2

FLOWER FRAGRANCE

MATERIALS

Rectangular glass container, dry foam, pot pourri, plastic prongs, florist's clay. Dried rosebuds, dried lavender, dried larkspur, eucalyptus, preserved and bleached.

1 The rectangular glass container is fitted with pieces of dry foam, cut to leave a gap around each side. The space is filled in with a sprinkling of colourful and aromatic pot pourri.

2 Rosebuds and lavender, gathered into tiny bunches, form the basis of this charming countrified design in which the stems are all positioned vertically, an unusual way of using the plants.

3 Flashes of deep blue are provided by short-cut stems of larkspur and colour contrast by the sprays of preserved and bleached eucalyptus. This design would be suitable for a bedroom or guest room.

1

2

3

ARRANGEMENTS UNDER A GLASS DOME

A clear glass dome placed over an arrangement of dried flowers looks very effective and provides the additional benefit of protecting the flowers from dust.

Make the foundation for the arrangement out of foam or fine wire mesh formed to a suitable shape then insert flowers to build up an attractive display.

FLOWER CONE

Form fine wire mesh into a cone shape then fill it with foam. Seal the base of the cone with a circle of thin cardboard then stand it on a suitable base. Completely cover the cone with flowers.

HANGING ARRANGEMENTS

Use small garden hanging baskets packed with foam; or use a ball of dry foam covered completely with flowers. Push a hole right through it and thread through a toning ribbon with which to suspend the ball.

Shallow wicker or cane trays or baskets can be suspended by ribbons, fine rope or presentable thick twine, perhaps with different colours twined together and the flowers secured so they hang down over the edges. Some flowers could also be attached to the ribbons, rope or twine used to suspend the arrangement.

Wire coathangers, bent to shape and covered, can also form the base for suspended arrangements. Secure the flowers with florists' wire.

LAVENDER BOTTLES

Use lavender that is in full bloom and has long stems that are still supple. Pick 22 of them and tie the stems together firmly immediately below the flower heads with one end of a piece of ribbon .

ABOVE *Flower arrangement under a glass dome and flower cone.*

Turn the bunch upside down and bend the stems outwards and downwards gently so they form a sort of cage around the heads. Space the stems out in pairs. Weave the loose end of the ribbon over and under the stems until the heads are completely enclosed, weaving it rather tightly at the bottom and top, but more loosely in the centre so that it takes on a bottle shape. Wind the loose end of the ribbon firmly round the stems then tie in a firm bow. Trim the ends of the stems.

LEFT *A hanging flower arrangement.*

BELOW *A lavender bottle, traditionally made from lavender plaited with narrow ribbon to scent linen.*

THE LANGUAGE OF FLOWERS

Acacia – *secret love*
Almond blossom – *hope*
Amaryllis – *pride, splendid beauty*
Anemone – *forsaken*
Apple blossom – *preference*
Bell flower, white – *gratitude*
Bluebell – *constancy*
Broom – *humility*
Camellia, red – *unpretending excellence*
Camellia, white – *perfected excellence*
Carnation, red – *alas for my poor heart*
Carnation, striped – *refusal*
Chamomile – *patience*
Chrysanthemum, red – *I love*
Clematis – *mental beauty, purity*
Columbine – *folly*
Daisy – *innocence*
Elderflower – *compassion, consolation*
Everlasting flower – *unfading memory*
Forget-me-not – *fidelity, true love*
Hawthorn blossom – *hope*
Heartsease – *remembrance*
Hibiscus – *delicate beauty*
Honeysuckle – *devotion*
Hyacinth – *unobtrusive loveliness*
Hyacinth, blue – *constancy*
Jasmine, white – *amiability*
Jasmine, yellow – *happiness, grace and elegance*
Jonquil – *I desire a return of affection*

Lavender – *silence*
Lilac, purple – *first emotions of love*
Lilac, white – *youthful innocence*
Lily – *purity*
Lily of the valley – *purity, return of happiness*
Magnolia – *grief*
Marigold – *joy*
Michaelmas daisy – *farewell*
Mignonette – *your qualities are supreme*
Nasturtium – *patriotism*
Orange blossom – *purity and loveliness*
Pansies – *love, thought*
Peony – *bashfulness*
Pinks – *love*
Poppy, red – *consolation*
Primrose – *early youth*
Rose – *love*
Rose, musk – *capricious beauty*
Rosebud – *pure and lovely*
Rosemary – *remembrance*
Snowdrop – *hope*
Stock – *lasting beauty*
Sweet William – *gallantry*
Tulip – *love*
Violet – *modesty*
Wallflower – *fidelity in adversity*
Zinnia – *thoughts of absent friends*

INDEX